AMERICAN TREASURES IN THE LIBRARY OF CONGRESS

Harry N. Abrams, Inc., Publishers in association with the Library of Congress

Memory ☆ *Reason* ☆ *Imagination*

AMERICAN TREASURES IN THE LIBRARY OF CONGRESS

Introduction by Garry Wills

FOR HARRY N. ABRAMS, INC.:
Project Manager: Eric Himmel
Editor: Rachel Tsutsumi
Designer: Robert McKee

FOR THE LIBRARY OF CONGRESS:
Editor: Margaret E. Wagner
Coordinator of Photography: Blaine Marshall

Library of Congress Cataloging-in-Publication Data
American treasures in the Library of Congress:
memory/reason/imagination.
p.   cm.
Includes bibliographical references (p.   ) and index.
ISBN 0–8109–4298–4 (clothbound)
———— Copy3 Z663 .A8375 1997
I. United States—Civilization—Sources—Exhibitions.   2. Library of Congress—Exhibitions.
I. Library of Congress.
E173.A758 1997
973—dc21   96–48126

Photograph Credits
All of the photographs in this book were taken by Roger Foley except for the following:
Michael Dersin: pp. 2, 8; Toni Frissell: p. 163; William Gottlieb: p. 135; Jim Higgins: pp. 26, 86,
89, 93, 139, 155, 156, 160; Library of Congress: pp. 29, 42, 57, 64, 71, 78 (top), 97, 98, 102, 119,
151; Patrick Loughney: pp. 54, 152; Ed Owen: pp. 72, 73, 121; Merrilee Love Wilson: p. 101.

"Something's Coming" (p. 138) from *West Side Story* by Leonard Bernstein and Stephen Sondheim.
Copyright © 1956, 1957 (renewed) by Leonard Bernstein and Stephen Sondheim. The Leonard
Bernstein Music Publishing Company LLC U.S. and Canadian publisher, G. Schirmer, Inc.
Worldwide print rights and Publisher for the rest of the World. Used by Permission.

Title page: Main Reading Room, Thomas Jefferson Building, Library of Congress
Page 8: Minerva, *a marble mosaic by Elihu Vedder in the Great Hall of*
the Thomas Jefferson Building, Library of Congress

☆ *Contents* ☆

FOREWORD
by James H. Billington
6

LETTER FROM PAUL A. ALLAIRE
9

INTRODUCTION: NATIONAL TREASURES
by Garry Wills
10

MEMORY
16

REASON
58

IMAGINATION
116

BUILDING THE NATIONAL COLLECTION
by Abby Smith
164

PRESERVING THE PAST
166

OBJECT LIST
168

INDEX
173

F O R E W O R D

The Library of Congress began in 1800 as a small collection of books and documents that Congress used as its reference library in drafting legislation for the fledgling republic. Now, nearly two hundred years later, Congress still turns to its Library for information when debating and drafting laws. But the Library that supports Congress has also expanded to comprise nearly 110 million items, in all formats, from ancient Sumerian tablets to magnetic tape, from sixteenth-century maps and the papers of twenty-three presidents to the early movies of Thomas Edison and CD-ROM versions of modern encyclopedias. And in between are all sorts of once-new technologies, such as daguerreotypes, wire recordings, and wax cylinders, which have long ago been superseded by even newer ones.

The Library of Congress houses the Copyright Office of the United States, and the Library selects some 800,000 books, maps, and other items deposited here each year for copyright for inclusion in its research collections. This is one of the important ways in which it collects a living record of American history and creative achievement. The Library has been built and sustained by Congress for its constituents and thus serves not only as a congressional library, but also as the national library of the United States.

Moreover, because America's roots are in foreign lands and its interests are worldwide, this library has international holdings unmatched by any other institution. We have the largest collection of items in Russian outside of Russia and of Japanese literature outside of Japan, to name just two examples. But we are also unique among the world's national libraries in that we allow all adults to use the collections for research purposes, without demanding special permission or accreditation from a university or other institution. We are open to all researchers over the age of eighteen, and now, through our special commitment to make our key American history collections available in digital form on the Internet, we will reach both students and researchers all over the country and, indeed, the globe.

As we make our collections accessible through electronic means, we are also making available our rarest and most significant holdings to visitors of all ages by opening for the first time a permanent exhibition of *Treasures of the Library of Congress.* The Library will begin this exhibition by displaying scores of priceless original American documents: the handwritten letters and diaries of Washington, Jefferson, Lincoln, and Roosevelt; the first extant American photograph of the human face; unrealized designs for the U.S. Capitol; Maya Lin's sketches for the Vietnam Veterans Memorial; the laboratory notebooks of Alexander Graham Bell; manuscripts by Walt Whitman and Robert Frost; musical scores by Irving Berlin, John Philip Sousa, and Aaron Copland; sketches by Orson Welles and Frank Lloyd Wright; and the first dime novel and one of the earliest baseball cards ever produced.

All of this is made possible through the generous support of The Document Company, Xerox. We share a common vision of the importance of original documents, and Xerox is providing special funds for preserving the fragile originals of special treasures for display in a state-of-the-art exhibit case that will protect them from environmental and security risks. Each item displayed in this constantly changing exhibit will be an item found to be both intrinsically interesting and historically significant by the Library's staff of curators, who are responsible for building our collections and serving them to the public. With their intimate knowledge of the Library's vast collections, the curators are the living link between the creator and the user.

In this volume, each item is seen through the curators' eyes. The book focuses on special treasures from our rich holdings of Americana and captures only a small sampling of what will be available here at the Thomas Jefferson Building in coming years. In acknowledgment of our debt to Jefferson, whose personal collection of 6,487 volumes became the core of today's Library of Congress, the book has been organized according to the categories he used to catalog his own books. We invite you to visit the Library when you are in Washington, D.C., and to visit the exhibition on-line at http://www.loc.gov.

JAMES H. BILLINGTON
THE LIBRARIAN OF CONGRESS

Throughout our nation's history, certain key documents—the Declaration of Independence, the Emancipation Proclamation, the Gettysburg Address—have shaped our thoughts, recorded our progress, and expressed our highest ideals as a nation. The Library of Congress has the original handwritten drafts of these documents among its vast holdings, as well as other material that embodies great creative achievements in the arts and sciences.

A nation's history always includes a compilation of documents, and as The Document Company, Xerox is pleased to join the Library of Congress in a special partnership to preserve this unique record of our common heritage and make it available to the public in the *Treasures of the Library of Congress* exhibition, a permanent exhibition opening in May 1997.

If a nation is to survive, each generation must learn from the ones before it. And so we at Xerox share the vision of the Founding Fathers, who made the establishment of a library for Congress among the first priorities of the young nation after moving the capital to the District of Columbia. They knew that enlightened government depends on the vigilance and zeal of enlightened people. As James Madison said, "Knowledge will forever govern ignorance: and a people who mean to be their own governours, must arm themselves with the power which knowledge gives." We know that a sound and vibrant democracy can flourish only among a people with free and unfettered access to information.

As a corporation that values learning and knowledge, we also share the educational vision of the Library and this exhibit: that people's lives can be enriched and improved by closer contact with the original words and images of those who came before us and aspired to the same ideals we do. Through our support of the *Treasures of the Library of Congress* exhibition and its various outreach programs, we help to preserve and exhibit these treasures, and to ensure that our nation's cultural heritage is accessible to one and all, now and in the future.

PAUL A. ALLAIRE
CHAIRMAN OF THE BOARD AND CHIEF EXECUTIVE OFFICER
OF XEROX AND PRESIDENT OF THE XEROX FOUNDATION

NATIONAL TREASURES

It is the duty of every good citizen to use all the opportunities which occur to him for preserving documents relating to the history of our country.

—THOMAS JEFFERSON, 1823[1]

I suppose that few of us can claim to have met Jefferson's test of "every good citizen," collecting the materials of our country's history. Luckily, the Library of Congress (with other institutions) does much of this for us. We can enjoy the fruits of citizenship, in this area, while doing few of the labors.

But why does Jefferson—the great progressive among the founders, a man so optimistic about the future—call for such intense effort to preserve the past? Should we not be looking forward rather than backward? In Jefferson's revolutionary time, America was breaking free from the past, throwing off its shackles, confident of a glorious future. But the future is, by definition, what does not exist in the present. It will be generated out of us, out of our ideals or hopes or determination, only insofar as the past has forged those qualities in us. To forget the past is to lose identity. This is what makes movies about amnesia so dramatic. If the protagonist does not know what he did yesterday, he cannot know who he is today.

Such amnesia can afflict whole cultures as well as individuals. The Czech novelist, Milan Kundera, fashioned a parable about this in *The Unbearable Lightness of Being* (1984). During the "Prague Spring" of 1968, when Soviet tanks invade Czechoslovakia, resisters take down street signs to confuse the enemy forces and render their city maps useless. But after the uprising is put down, and the novel's heroine goes back to familiar places, she finds new street names put up by the conquerors, weakening the places' connections with her identity. She can no longer orient herself to her own past, which leaves her adrift in the present.

---

1. Jefferson to Hugh P. Taylor, 4 October 1823, *The Writings of Thomas Jefferson*, ed. A. A. Lipscomb and A. E. Bergh (Washington, D.C.: Thomas Jefferson Memorial Association of the United States, 1903–4), 15:473.

Precisely *because* the United States was forging its own ethos as a new form of government, Jefferson insisted on preserving every bit of evidence that showed how this experiment in history came to be made. He collected not only books by and about the American past. He acquired manuscripts, documents, maps, court records, all kinds of evidence—about Native Americans, about the continental flora and fauna, about archaeological finds and specimens. His care to preserve these was so great that he would not risk sending legal manuscripts to his old law teacher, a short distance away in Williamsburg, where George Wythe was writing about Virginia's laws. Wythe would have to come to Jefferson, since some documents were "so rotten that in turning a leaf it sometimes falls into powder."[2]

Jefferson used the most advanced conservation techniques available to him: "These I preserve by wrapping and sewing them in oil cloth, so that neither air nor moisture can have access to them."[3] When Jefferson sold his extensive library to the nation, to reestablish a library for Congress's use after the Capitol was burnt in the War of 1812, he passed on the duty of preserving the evidence of our history to our elected representatives.

Jefferson's books were first catalogued in Congress according to his own tripartite system, arranged according to the faculties of the mind—history (for the mind's *memory*), philosophy (for *reason*), and the arts (for *imagination*). The same categories have been used to arrange this catalogue of special treasures from the huge collection that Jefferson's original library has grown to include.

In a sense, everything in the Library is special. It is all a testimony to the nation's life. Jefferson collected and preserved newspapers as well as classic books of theory. He had volumes of eighteen different newspapers bound for future historians' use.[4] Often a library's most useful future possessions are things that seemed trivial at the time of their appearance.

------

2. Jefferson to George Wythe, 16 January 1796, Lipscomb and Bergh, *Writings*, 9:319.

3. Ibid.

4. Millicent Sowerby, *Catalogue of the Library of Thomas Jefferson* (Washington, D.C.: Library of Congress, 1952), 1:267–85.

We generally and loosely think of a library as a repository of *books*, written by *authors*—a place, as John Ruskin said, where we go to commune with great minds speaking through great works. A library is that, of course— among other things. But sometimes we go to a library to consult *things*, not authors—maps, reports, genealogies, old calendars, school yearbooks, laws, church records, election polls. These can affect our knowledge of our own family, the plats of land we live on or cultivate, the government we live under. Yes, we go at times to find Plato in the library. But we also go to find ourselves, in the weave of testimonials to the past that formed us. And a historical collection, one that looks for a whole community's roots, will have many kinds of evidence—not only what was written about an election, for instance, but the posters and "broadside" handout sheets that reflect what voters actually saw and used in that election, and even the campaign ribbons of the candidates.

It may surprise some that campaign ribbons are among the treasures of a library—or, more amazing, that the contents of President Lincoln's pockets on the night when he was murdered are here, part of a bequest by Lincoln's granddaughter. These items are not only poignant reminders of the individual who owned them, but samples of what a prominent man of Lincoln's time would carry with him—glasses and a knife of American manufacture, the odd souvenir (Confederate money), an embroidered handkerchief. A moment in the cultural life of Lincoln's time is frozen here, along with a sad reminder of his death.

Jefferson knew the importance of evidence that goes beyond the written word. In the home that housed his library, he had not only the reports of the Lewis and Clark expedition he himself dispatched to the West, but materials they brought back with them; not only his refutation of Europe's claims about American animal remains, but the bones of a no-longer-extant "mammoth"; not only carefully collected samples of Native American dialects, but a large Indian painting on a buffalo hide; not only architectural drawings and textbooks, but engravings of finished buildings (including Mount Vernon). Monticello was a fully integrated and didactic assemblage of Americana reflecting the experience of the entire country up to Jefferson's time. Even the library at Monticello, in which Jefferson worked, had a historical item that he worked *in*—the chair from which he had presided over the Senate as a vice-president. That part of his library was not sold to Congress since Jefferson was still using it. But in bequests of published and written materials now, such artifacts are often included as part of the collection to be sent on after the owner's death.

In this collection, as in any representation of American culture and its past, what must astound is the immense diversity of our nation. By European standards, the United States stretches over a forbiddingly vast territory, one to be filled up by people from different countries and ethnic backgrounds, speaking different languages, practicing different religions. Some thought the country would be too heterogeneous to cohere. The multiplicity affected our national character, our laws, our institutions. Because of it, we did not, like all preceding Western cultures, have an established national religion. Because of it, we have a two-party system based on compromise and inclusion, not a parliamentary system of focused ideologies. (Doctrinal parties work in ethnically homogenous societies like Israel, India, or Great Britain. In our heterogeneous society they would prove divisive.)

It is natural, then, that one's first impression of the Library's exhibited treasures should be jumbled and disparate. Here we have things apparently incommensurate—comic books and the Declaration of Independence, the design for a macaroni machine and the design for the United States Capitol, a cookbook and the Gettysburg Address. Wandering in this cavern of the national memories is like fumbling through the dark places of our individual past, as that fumbling was described by Saint Augustine:

> *I reach the lawns and spacious structures of memory, where treasures are stored—all the images conveyed there by any of our senses, and, moreover, all the ideas derived by expanding, contracting, or otherwise manipulating the images; everything ticketed, here, and stored for preservation (everything that has not been blotted out, in the interval, and buried in oblivion). Some things, summoned, are instantly delivered up, though others require a longer search, to be drawn from recesses less penetrable. And all the while jumbled memories flirt out on their own, interrupting the search for what we want, pestering: "Wasn't it us you were seeking?" My heart strenuously waves these things off from my memory's gaze until the dim thing sought arrives, at last, fresh from depths. Yet other things are summoned up in easy sequence, linked things passing in sequence, to be laid back in the same order, recallable at will—which happens whenever I recite a passage from memory.*[5]

What binds together disparate things in our personal memory is the intimate connection of them all with our own life. And the more one moves about among the treasures of the Library of Congress, the more ties one begins to feel between each item and the nation's life story. Finding such connections is a rewarding personal challenge.

Early comic books, for instance, remind us what a visual culture ours has been, even before the television age. This forms a link between the comics and Theodore Roosevelt's letter to his son, which tells a story partly in pictures; and it takes us even further back, to the "Hieroglyphick Bible" that made the most sacred stories available to children. That Bible is the ancestor of the "classic comics" I read in my childhood (*Moby Dick* was more memorable for me in that format than in the movie later made with Gregory Peck). If you have any doubt that a simply drawn visual image can have great power, just look at Paul Conrad's "cartoon" on Justice Thurgood Marshall's death, which powerfully fuses the idea of permanent architecture and the image of a fallen tree in the forest, stability and fragility joined in a wrenching paradox. All these things are, in a sense, descendants of the pictograph Indian buffalo hide at Monticello.

---

5. Saint Augustine, *Confessions* 10.8.

Other connections almost force themselves upon us—the mingled kinds of music to which our country has always moved: hymns, war songs, Native American flute music, African-American jazz, Broadway shows. The civil rights leader Andrew Young wrote that "freedom songs" kept demonstrators united and hopeful during the marches that were pelted with rocks, obscenities, and spittle. America has always moved forward to the accompaniment of its freedom songs, not only Sousa marches but songs like Leonard Bernstein's "Something's Coming," a typically American combination of the hesitant and the plunging when Americans look to the future.

An equally persistent theme is that of law. Ours is one of the modern world's first written constitutions. And law is something everyone can resort to in our litigious society. Thurgood Marshall was famous for pleading and winning cases in the Supreme Court long before he took his seat on that bench. The cases of Susan B. Anthony and of William Gobitis [sic] show how private citizens can take the rights of women or religious minorities before the nation's tribunals.

Another thing that must haunt any representative collection of Americana is space. Our patriotic song gets it right: "Oh beautiful for spacious skies." The sheer extent of the American continent was hard to comprehend, even as its reach was being revealed in things like the Lewis and Clark voyage of discovery, or the Louisiana Purchase that doubled the area of the United States. The lure of westward lands led to the glorification of "the frontier," and to a nature mysticism seen in the paintings and photographs of the continent's natural beauties—Yellowstone and Yosemite and Grand Canyon, or Black Canyon as it is seen in this collection.

Maps were not only instruments of knowledge but of power to the growing nation. Expansion came by way of land speculation, which involved careful checking of territorial rights, legal claims, and investment areas. Many a young American based his later career on a period as surveyor. George Washington surveyed not only the nascent city of Alexandria, Virginia, but whole tracts west of the Blue Ridge Mountains. A sense of the wonder of the American landscape can be gained not only from paintings by a Bierstadt or a Church but from the topographical map created by Hal Shelton, which demonstrates the aesthetic quality of scientific precision applied to cartography.

I said earlier that everything related to our national history can be considered a treasure—which was

Jefferson's view. But treasure is used in a more restricted sense for the purposes of this exhibit. It refers to things of more obvious or immediate interest. Take, for instance, the collection of scheduled programs for NBC radio. That is a rich trove for people studying the years reported on by NBC news, or for cultural historians interested in the history of American taste (in music, comedy, and drama), or for historians of radio technology and corporate growth. Those are relatively specialized interests for most of us. But we can all feel the drama implicit in one such daybook—that for December 7, 1941. This shows us how the nation learned, gradually and by ever more stunning reports, of an attack on Pearl Harbor that would tear across the tissue of our lives, just as it intruded on, scrambled, and made irrelevant all the planned programming that had to be sacrificed to urgent bulletins by NBC.

Insurance documents seem very dry things in general. But they are often the key to vital parts of our past. My historian son established the date of a plantation house on display at the Henry Ford Museum from a neglected insurance document in Maryland. Maps of insured areas and structures allow us to call up the shape of things past—including the Tombstone plat on which the O.K. Corral, of shoot-out fame, is traceable. In this case, a document pins down to hard historical reality a tale that could otherwise float off into realms of mere fancy or legend.

We tend to treat as special—a treasure in that sense—early samples of what became a regular part of later life: the ancestor of the baseball card, for instance, or early comics. Or the first edition of a book like *The Wizard of Oz*, which has become as fixed in our psyche as ancestral legend, so that we need to be reminded that it had a specific beginning in the mind of a single author (not a whole "Folk"). The Library of Congress is especially strong on such "firsts," since it keeps the records of copyright applications.

If it is interesting to see the start of a series of things, it is even more amazing to see the faltering origins of unique things—to see Jefferson fumbling his way toward the lapidary statement of rights in the Declaration of Independence, or to see an early draft of Lincoln's Gettysburg Address, a draft that has almost (but not quite) achieved the final polish we know from books, or to look at the first form of what would become the Emancipation Proclamation. We are present at the creation when we look at these marks, made by a hand still listening for the mind's last precisions. It is a genetic *process* we stare at, not just an inert page.

☆ *Memory* ☆

All the items in this collection are historical in the broad sense. They are markers from our past. The songs are part of the history of art, the laws are part of the history of government. But Jefferson took "history" in a more restricted sense when he set up his first category of things principally to be *remembered*. Individual events are the stuff of history, according to Aristotle, concrete happenings, not philosophical abstractions or artistic symbolizations (Jefferson's three categories are already there in Aristotle).[1] Here we can see religious communities articulating their early efforts on this continent—Puritans publishing the country's first book (a Psalter), Jews expressing their devotion to the new country led by President Washington, German Pietists creating a hymnal that eventually came into the possession of Benjamin Franklin. Here are memorable things from political campaigns—or military campaigns. We see Custer, not at the Battle of the Little Bighorn, where he died, but in the Civil War, where he earned the fame put at risk in the West. The Flagg poster from World War I became one of the most famous icons of our past. The costume that Orson Welles designed for his production of *Doctor Faustus* (mounted when he was twenty-two years old) is not simply an artifact from theatrical lore. It represents an important moment in the New Deal's history, since Welles (and his partner John Houseman) were doing work for the Federal Theatre Project. In fact, they called their production company at the time Project 891, after the number of the Works Progress Administration subsidy for the theater.[2]

The preservation of the Welles production items as part of the WPA records is an example of the way mere government records can enclose, like a fly in amber, a whole event or experience from the

---

1. Aristotle, *Poetics* 51a36–b15.

2. David Thomson, *Rosebud: The Story of Orson Welles* (New York: Alfred A. Knopf, 1996), 64.

past. The careful ordering of such materials provides a stunning foil to the disorder and chaos of the hero's vast possessions in Welles's great movie, *Citizen Kane*. The clues to a man's past go up in fire at that picture's end, a symbol of disorderly memory reflecting a disorderly life—a life devoted to sheer acquisition without the sorting and evaluating that shape an identity by articulating one's surroundings.

The exhibit that perhaps best encapsulates the historical role of the Library collection is that which shows Groucho Marx boasting of the fact that the Library of Congress had asked for his papers—papers that are an invaluable store of information on the many arts Marx mastered (vaudeville, Broadway, movies, radio, and television) and the many people he dealt with over the years. The clip from *The Tonight Show* with Johnny Carson is itself a historical document illustrating how the Library creates and updates its materials, and then records that process as it is reflected in the popular culture.

For those of us who have warm memories of both Groucho Marx and Johnny Carson, this television moment marks a point where our personal memories and the national collection intersect. By doing this, it vividly represents the encounter between the personal and the national, the private and the public, that occurs constantly in exposure to these treasures—the sifting and revaluing of things in our memory that give us the tools for self-criticism and for envisioning our own contributions to the store of national initiatives. If we cannot all, like Jefferson, collect materials that register the nation's history, we can all appreciate the results of that process—and then make some history of our own. Whatever we make of our own time, the Library will be there to record and remember it.

G. WILLS

AMERICA'S FIRST BOOK

This humble and well-worn hymnal was printed in 1640 in Cambridge, Massachusetts, by Stephen Daye, first printer of the Massachusetts Bay Colony. It is the very first book printed in what is now the United States. Known as *The Bay Psalm Book*, but really titled *The Whole Booke of Psalmes Faithfully Translated into English Metre*, it represents what was most sacred to the Puritans—a faithful translation of God's Word, to be sung in worship by the entire congregation. Other Protestant denominations relied on selected paraphrases of the Scripture, but the Puritans believed this could compromise their salvation. The same faith that compelled them to leave England and strike out for the New World prompted them to commit this text to print before all others.

Like any book that is used every day, *The Bay Psalm Book* suffered much handling over time. One of only eleven copies known to have survived to the present day, this volume was first saved, about 1700, by a book collector, then a student at Harvard College, who later gave his library, including this book, to Old South Church in Boston. There it lay in the church steeple, half-forgotten, until the mid nineteenth century, when the cash-strapped church sold it to Bible collector George Livermore. In 1894, businessman, philanthropist, and book collector Alfred White purchased it at auction. It was donated to the Library of Congress in 1966 by his daughter, Annie Jean Van Sinderen, who recognized that America's national library would not be complete without a copy of America's first book. This copy takes its place at the head of the American Imprint Collection at the Library, which represents almost half of the nearly forty thousand works published in our country before 1801.

SINGING FOR SALVATION

The principal source for the music of the German Seventh-Day Baptists, a group that immigrated to Pennsylvania in 1732, this manuscript is inscribed with a title that unrolls in the full proliferation of German Pietism: "The Bitter good, or the song of the lonesome turtledove, the Christian church here on earth, in the valley of sadness, where it bemoans its 'widowhood' and at the same time sings of another, future reunion [with God]."

Johann Conrad Beissel, founder of the Seventh-Day Baptists, served not only as spiritual director of the group but also as its composer, devising his own system of composition. His method is described in chapter eight of Thomas Mann's 1947 novel *Doktor Faustus*:

> *He decreed that there should be "masters" and "servants" in every scale . . . And those syllables upon which the accent lay had always to be presented by a "master," the unaccented by a "servant."*

With these rules Beissel set to music the hymn texts of his denomination (many of which he had written) and large passages of the Bible. He is said to have hoped to set the entire Bible to music in this system. In performance his music seems almost willfully awkward to those accustomed to normal German hymnody—or even to the homegrown hymntunes of the late-eighteenth-century English-language American tunesmiths—but the passionate need to express the words of the text is never in doubt. This style of music declined after Beissel's death in 1768.

The group's illuminated musical manuscripts were hand-lettered in Fraktur and are among the earliest original music composed in the British colonies. This volume was once in the possession of Benjamin Franklin, and a note on the flyleaf reads: "April 1775. This curious book was lent me by Doctor Franklin just before he set out for Pennsylvania."

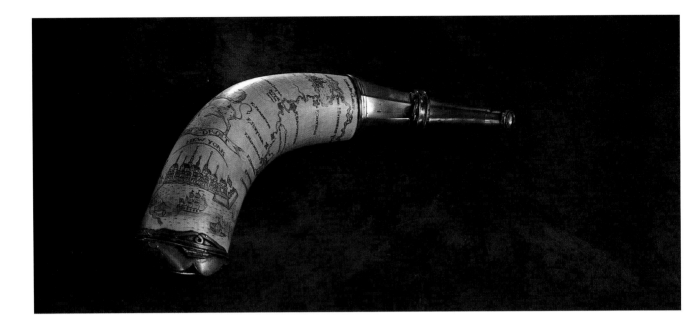

AN INDISPENSABLE COMPANION

One of the most fascinating cartographic formats represented in the Library's holdings is a collection of eight powder horns inscribed with maps, dating from the time of the French and Indian War and the American Revolutionary War. For soldiers, hunters, or frontiersmen in the late colonial period, powder horns were indispensable companions to their muskets. Fashioned out of cow or ox horns, they made convenient containers for carrying and protecting gunpowder. Usually handmade, these horns were often inscribed with rhymes, references to particular campaigns, names of forts or towns, diary entries, or maps. Since maps were scarce during the time period, it is possible that map-inscribed powder horns served as guides for their owners, but it is more likely that the map images provided records or mementos of the areas that the owners traversed or the campaigns in which they were involved.

The powder horn shown here is undated and unsigned, although it is believed to date from between 1757 and 1760. It shows the Hudson and Mohawk River valleys, as well as Lake Champlain and Lake Ontario, waterways that served as the major arteries of travel between New York City (portrayed pictorially at the bottom of the horn) and the St. Lawrence River Valley to the north, and the Great Lakes to the west. Numerous towns and forts along the route are named, and houses, windmills, boats, and other details enliven the design. The horn also bears a British coat of arms, suggesting the owner was an American colonial or British soldier.

This powder horn is part of the Peter Force Collection, which the Library of Congress purchased by an act of Congress in 1867. Force (1790–1868) was the preeminent collector of Americana (including maps) during the first half of the nineteenth century.

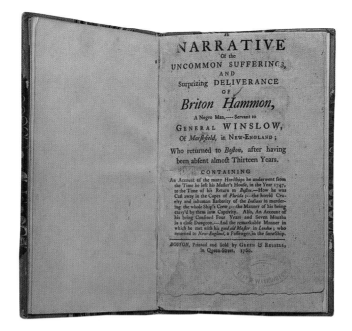

A NARRATIVE OF UNCOMMON SUFFERINGS

This first slave narrative independently printed in the North American colonies recounts the adventures of Briton Hammon (fl. 1760) during an extended absence from his master, which included a shipwreck off the Florida capes, captivity among cannibalistic Indians, imprisonment by pirates in Havana, and service on several British gun ships, one of which saw action against the French. Told in the picaresque style of the popular "rake's progress" literature, this tale is representative of the early slave narrative genre and at the same time an example of another popular genre—captivity tales:

> As soon as the Vessel was burnt down to the Water's edge, the Indians stood for the Shore, together with our Boat, on board of which they put 5 hands. After we came to the Shore, they led me to their Hutts, where I expected nothing but immediate Death, and as they spoke broken English, were often telling me, while coming from the Sloop to the Shore, that they intended to roast me alive. But the Providence of God order'd it otherways, for He appeared for my Help, in this Mount of Difficulty, and they were better to me than my Fears, and soon unbound me, but set a Guard over me every Night.

This copy is one of only two known extant and was formerly in the great Americana library of the nineteenth-century collector George Brinley of Hartford, Connecticut.

Among the nearly six thousand known slave narratives, the Library has significant examples of all types, including eighteenth-century pieces published separately for slave or former-slave authors, those published with the aid of nineteenth-century abolitionist editors, and an extensive compilation of ex-slave testimonials by the Works Progress Administration's Federal Writers' Project in the 1930s.

GENERAL WASHINGTON TAKES COMMAND

George Washington (1732–1799), leader of the revolutionary movement in Virginia and a former British colonial army officer, was commissioned "commander-in-chief of the army of the United Colonies of all the forces raised and to be raised by them" on June 19, 1775, by delegates at the Continental Congress. The commission is written on vellum and signed by John Hancock of Massachusetts, president of the Continental Congress, and by Charles Thomson of Pennsylvania, secretary of the Continental Congress.

General Washington had been formally appointed commander in chief on June 15, 1775. The four-day difference between his appointment and his commission date is due to the lengthy preparation of the document. While other men, such as John Hancock himself, may have entertained hopes of receiving the appointment, General Washington was reluctant, writing to his wife, Martha, in a June 18, 1775, letter: "You may believe me my dear Patsy, when I assure you in the most solemn manner, that, so far from seeking this appointment, I have used every endeavor in my power to avoid it." Nevertheless, Washington set out immediately to take command of the American army that was besieging the British forces in Boston, Massachusetts.

In Congress

The delegates of the United Colonies of New-Hampshire, Massachusetts bay, Rhode-Island, Connecticut, New York, New-Jersey, Pennsylvania, New-Castle, Kent & Sussex in Delaware, Maryland, Virginia, North-Carolina & South Carolina

To George Washington Esquire

We reposing especial trust and confidence in your patriotism, conduct and fidelity DO by these presents constitute and appoint you to be General and Commander in chief of the army of the United Colonies and of all the forces raised or to be raised by them and of all others who shall voluntarily offer their service and join the said army for the defence of American liberty and for repelling every hostile invasion thereof And you are hereby vested with full power and authority to act as you shall think for the good and welfare of the service. And we do hereby strictly charge and require all officers and soldiers under your command to be obedient to your orders and diligent in the exercise of their several duties. And we do also enjoin and require you to be careful in executing the great trust reposed in you, by causing strict discipline and order to be observed in the army, and that the soldiers are duly exercised and provided with all convenient necessaries. And you are to regulate your conduct in every respect by the rules and discipline of war (as herewith given you) and punctually to observe and follow such orders and directions from time to time as you shall receive from this or a future Congress of the said United Colonies or committee of Congress for that purpose appointed.

This Commission to continue in force until revoked by this or a future Congress.

Dated Philadelphia June 19th 1775.

Attest. Cha Thomson Secy

By order of the Congress,

John Hancock President

To the President of the United States of America.

Sir

Permit the children of the Stock of Abraham to approach you with the most cordial affection and esteem for your person & merits—and to join with our fellow citizens in welcoming you to NewPort.

With pleasure we reflect on those days—those days of difficulty & danger when the God of Israel who delivered David from the peril of the sword,—shielded Your head in the day of battle:—and we rejoice to think, that the same Spirit, who rested in the Bosom of the greatly beloved Daniel enabling him to preside over the Provinces of the Babylonish Empire, rests and ever will rest upon you, enabling you to discharge the arduous duties of Chief Magistrate in these States.

Deprived as we heretofore have been of the invaluable rights of free Citizens, we now with a deep sense of gratitude to the Almighty disposer of all events behold a Government, erected by the Majesty of the People—a Government, which to bigotry gives no sanction, to persecution no assistance—but generously affording to All liberty of conscience, and immunities of Citizenship: deeming every one, of whatever Nation, tongue, or language, equal parts of the great governmental Machine:—This so ample and extensive Federal Union whose basis is Philanthropy, Mutual confidence and Public Virtue, we cannot but acknowledge to be the work of the Great God, who ruleth in the Armies of Heaven and among the Inhabitants of the Earth, doing whatsoever seemeth him good.

For all the Blessings of civil and religious liberty which we enjoy under an equal and benign administration, we desire to send up our thanks to the Antient of Days, the great preserver of Men—beseeching him, that the Angel who conducted our forefathers through the wilderness into the promised land, may graciously conduct you through all the difficulties and dangers of this mortal life:—And, when like Joshua full of days and full of honour, you are gathered to your Fathers, may you be admitted into the Heavenly Paradise to partake of the water of life, and the tree of immortality.

Done and Signed by Order of the Hebrew Congregation in NewPort Rhode Island August 17th 1790:

Moses Seixas Warden

"TO BIGOTRY NO SANCTION, TO PERSECUTION NO ASSISTANCE"

This congratulatory address, written by Moses Seixas (1744–1809), was presented by the Hebrew Congregation in Newport, Rhode Island, on behalf of "the children of the stock of Abraham" to President George Washington on August 17, 1790, on the occasion of his visit to the city. In his address, Seixas referred to past persecutions of the Jews and then lauded the new nation's commitment to religious liberty:

> *Deprived as we heretofore have been of the invaluable rights of free citizens, we now (with a deep sense of gratitude to the Almighty disposer of all events) behold a government erected by the Majesty of the People—a Government which to bigotry gives no sanction, to persecution no assistance, but generously affording to All liberty of conscience and immunities of Citizenship, deeming every one, of whatever Nation, tongue, or language, equal parts of the great governmental machine.*

In his reply, President Washington echoed Seixas's words:

> *It is now no more that toleration is spoken of as if it was the indulgence of one class of people that another enjoyed the exercise of their inherent natural rights. For happily, the government of the United States, which gives to bigotry no sanction, to persecution no assistance, requires only that they who live under its protection should demean themselves as good citizens, in giving it on all occasions their effectual support.*

These two letters were published in several newspapers that year and thus became the first presidential declaration of the free and equal status of Jews in America. Seixas's original formulation, "To bigotry . . . no sanction, to persecution no assistance," became—through its use by President Washington—a cherished expression of America's abiding commitment to safeguard the rights and freedoms of all its inhabitants.

FOR PRESIDENT, ABRAM LINCOLN

Use of the graphic arts to promote the aims of political parties and their candidates has a rich tradition in American history, and the 1860 presidential campaign was no exception. Brightly colored banners, outrageous political cartoons, sentimental sheet music covers, patriotic portraits, and visually stirring certificates of membership to rival political clubs were printed to sway individual voters and popular opinion. This bold campaign banner supports the candidacy of Abraham Lincoln (1809–1865) during his first (and victorious) presidential campaign in 1860. The flag was meant to hang like a banner in parades and other political spectacles, so that Lincoln's face would be oriented vertically. The printer liberally changed the spelling of Lincoln's first name ("Abram") to accommodate his design. The Library has a rich collection of graphic political ephemera, much of which, like this piece, came through copyright deposit.

"WE ARE NOT ENEMIES, BUT FRIENDS"

In composing his first inaugural address, delivered March 4, 1861, Abraham Lincoln focused on shoring up his support in the North without further alienating the South, where he was almost universally hated or feared. For guidance and inspiration, he turned to four historic documents, all concerned directly or indirectly with states' rights: Daniel Webster's 1830 reply to Robert Y. Hayne; President Andrew Jackson's Nullification Proclamation of 1832; Henry Clay's compromise speech of 1850; and the U.S. Constitution. His initial effort—two versions of its first and last pages shown here—was set in type and printed at the office of the *Illinois State Journal*. Though beautifully written, this "First Draft" of the address was perhaps too harsh for its intended purpose, a fact Lincoln may have recognized, for he readily accepted recommended changes from trusted friends and political advisors.

The finished address avoided any mention of the Republican Party platform, which condemned all efforts to reopen the African slave trade and denied the authority of Congress or a territorial legislature to legalize slavery in the territories. The address also denied any plan on the part of the Lincoln administration to interfere with the institution of slavery in states where it existed. But to Lincoln, the Union, which he saw as older even than the Constitution, was perpetual and unbroken, and secession legally impossible.

In the famous concluding paragraph Lincoln incorporated several changes proposed by William H. Seward, the future secretary of state. The style, however, is purely Lincoln's own:

I am loth to close. We are not enemies, but friends. We must not be enemies. Though passion may have strained, it must not break our bonds of affection. The mystic chords of memory, stre[t]ching from every battle-field, and patriot grave, to every living heart and hearthstone, all over this broad land, will yet swell the chorus of the Union, when again touched, as surely they will be, by the better angels of our nature.

The two surviving copies of the "First Draft" and four of the five known copies of the circulated draft are in the Robert Todd Lincoln Papers in the Library of Congress.

GEORGE CUSTER'S CIVIL WAR COMMAND

George Armstrong Custer (1839–1876), who lost his life but achieved immortality at the Battle of the Little Bighorn in June 1876, first became known for his military exploits on behalf of the Union army during the Civil War. He began the war as a second lieutenant assigned to the Second Cavalry and served at the Battle of Bull Run. His efforts during the Peninsular campaign in spring 1862 convinced Gen. George McClellan to add him to his staff, and by war's end Custer had become one of the most celebrated and decorated officers in the Northern army.

In fall 1864, now a colonel in the regular army and a major general of the volunteer corps, Custer took over the Third Cavalry Division in support of the Shenandoah Valley campaign led by Gen. Philip Sheridan. During the campaign, Sheridan's men forced Confederate troops from the valley, which served the South as a major source of produce and provisions, and proceeded to burn and destroy homes, farms, and fields full of crops as they returned North. Custer so distinguished himself during the campaign that his division was given a prominent role in pursuing Gen. Robert E. Lee's Confederate army as it fled from Richmond in April 1865. It was Custer who received the Confederate flag of truce, which led to Lee's surrender at Appomattox Court House on the morning of April 9.

This sketch of Custer's division retiring from Mount Jackson in the Shenandoah Valley on October 7, 1864, is by Alfred Waud. Recognized as the best of the Civil War sketch artists who drew the war for the nation's pictorial press, Waud could render a scene quickly and accurately, with an artist's eye for composition and a reporter's instinct for human interest. At a time when the shutter speed of cameras was not fast enough to capture action, the public's only glimpse of battle came from sketch artists. Waud's apparent courage under fire and passion for the men he depicted drew him dangerously close to the fighting, and his drawings portray more intimately than those by any other artist the drama and horror of this country's most devastating conflict.

the 3rd Custer div, on the 7th of Oct.

somewhere near ... ... retiring and burning the forage

ARTIFACTS OF ASSASSINATION

When Abraham Lincoln was shot at Ford's Theatre in Washington, D.C., on April 14, 1865, he was carrying two pairs of spectacles and a lens polisher, a pocketknife, a watch fob, a linen handkerchief, and a brown leather wallet containing a five-dollar Confederate note and nine newspaper clippings, including several favorable to the president and his policies. Given to his son Todd upon his death, these everyday items, which through association with tragedy had become like relics, were kept in the Lincoln family for over seventy years. They came to the Library in 1937 as part of the generous bequest of Lincoln's granddaughter, Mary Lincoln Isham, that included several books and daguerreotypes, a silver inkstand, and Mary Todd Lincoln's seed pearl necklace and matching bracelets.

It is quite unusual for the Library to keep personal artifacts among its holdings, and they were not put on display until 1976, when then Librarian of Congress Daniel Boorstin thought their exposure would humanize a man who had become "mythologically engulfed." But the availability of these artifacts has only piqued interest in the Lincoln myth—the contents of Lincoln's pockets have been among the items visitors to the Library most often ask to see.

One of the most complete representations of conspiracy literature as well as newspaper accounts of the assassination, like that in the *New York Times* displayed here, was assembled by Alfred Whital Stern. The most extensive collection of Lincolniana ever assembled by a private individual, Stern's important gift to the Library in 1953 included books, broadsides, paintings, photographs, medals, manuscripts, and memorabilia.

TOMBSTONE, ARIZONA

The O.K. Corral, where the notorious gunfight of the Earp brothers and Doc Holliday versus the Clanton gang took place on October 26, 1881, is shown (between 3rd and 4th Streets, bounded by Fremont on the north and Allen on the south) in this 1886 fire insurance map of Tombstone, Arizona. This map is one of over 700,000 fire insurance map sheets produced by the Sanborn Map Company for more than twelve thousand American cities and towns from the 1870s until the 1950s. These maps were prepared primarily to assist insurance underwriters in determining the risk involved in insuring individual properties.

During the first half of the nineteenth century, most fire insurance companies were small and based in a single city. Consequently, the underwriters could themselves examine properties they were about to insure. However, as insurance companies became larger and expanded their coverage to numerous cities, a mapping industry developed to support this need. The Sanborn Map Company of New York eventually came to dominate the insurance mapping business.

As the Tombstone map illustrates, fire insurance maps provide a block-by-block inventory of the buildings in the built-up or congested parts of towns. The outline or footprint of each building is indicated, and the buildings are color coded to show the construction material (pink for brick; yellow for wood; brown for adobe). Numbers inside the lower right corner of each building indicate how many stories the building had, while the numbers outside the building on the street front refer to the street addresses, allowing researchers to correlate these locations with census records and city directories. Individual dwellings are marked with "D" or "Dwg," but the residents or owners are not identified. Factories, businesses (such as hotels, saloons, and liveries), churches, schools, and other public buildings (city hall, assay office, and library) are labeled by name.

Today, fire insurance maps are used for a wide variety of research purposes including genealogy, urban history and geography, historical preservation, and environmental studies. The Library accumulated its unsurpassed collection of fire insurance maps primarily through copyright deposit. In addition, the Bureau of the Census transferred a set of maps updated with pasted-on corrections through the mid-1950s to the Library of Congress in 1967.

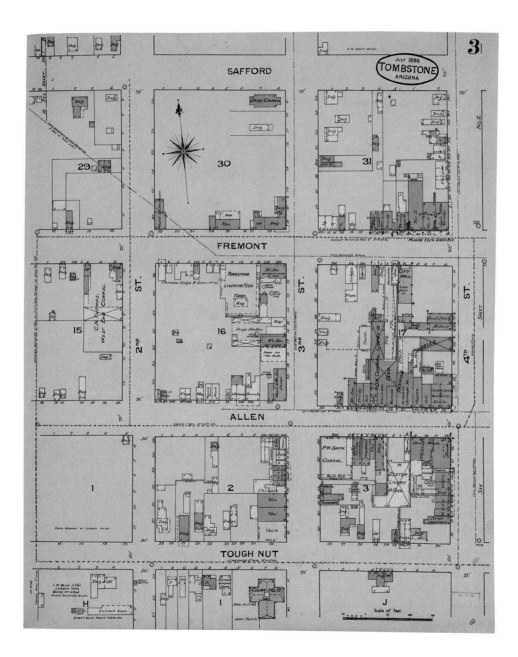

SAFFORD

JULY 1886
TOMBSTONE
ARIZONA

No. 2

EPISC. CHURCH

30

31

FREMONT

ST.

ST.

ST.

CITY HALL

C.N. THOMAS
WEST END CORRAL

TOMBSTONE
LIVERY & FEED

15

16

17

ALLEN

P.W. SMITH
CORRAL

1

2

3

DEXTER
LIVERY & FEED

TOUGH NUT

H

I

J

COURT HOUSE
JAIL

Scale of Feet.

37

RECORDING CULTURAL EXPRESSION

The first field recordings of Native American music contain Passamaquoddy songs, tales, and vocabulary, sung and spoken by Noel Josephs and Peter Selmore, as recorded by Jesse Walter Fewkes (1850–1930) at Calais, Maine, in mid-March 1890. The cylinder recording technique was patented by Thomas Edison in 1878, and by 1888 machines were becoming commercially available for use with prerecorded cylinders. But it was Fewkes, the man in the photograph, who first realized the potential of the cylinder recorder to revolutionize the methods of documenting human cultural expression. Knowing that he would participate in the Hemenway expedition to Hopi and Zuni pueblos in the Southwest during the summer of 1890, he decided to test the brand-new technology closer to his home in Boston. Delighted with the results, he immediately published enthusiastic accounts of the process and of his results in three journals, thereby spreading the word of the "talking machine's" utility to folklorists, linguists, ethnologists, and other interested parties. As he himself said on a cylinder recording in 1891, "You can talk into it as-fast-as-you-like, or you can speak a-s d-e-l-i-b-e-r-a-t-e-l-y a-s y-o-u c-h-o-o-s-e. In either case, it reproduces exactly what you say." This was significant because "the necessity of work with the phonograph in preserving the languages of the aborigines of this continent is imperative."

The two cylinders in the photograph are among those recorded in Maine between March 15 and 17, 1890. They came to the Library in 1970 from the Peabody Museum of Archaeology and Ethnology at Harvard University. The cylinder machine in the photo, while not the same model as Fewkes used, is a Columbia Graphophone, Model N, marketed in 1895 and manufactured in Washington, D.C.

A LETTER FROM THE PRESIDENT

Though the huggable "Teddy bear" was named after him, Theodore Roosevelt (1858–1919), who served as the president of the United States from 1901 to 1909, strove for a life that embodied his ideal of assertive masculinity. He was at various times an outdoor sportsman, explorer, western rancher, and soldier, as well as an aggressive political leader and writer on history and public affairs.

While the American people had ample opportunity to observe Roosevelt's public side, he kept his personal relationships extremely private. The letter reproduced here shows an aspect of Roosevelt's life seldom seen by the public.

Roosevelt established a residence in the nation's capital during his six years with the U.S. Civil Service Commission. But his family also spent time at Sagamore Hill, their Long Island residence, during Washington, D.C.'s sweltering summers in the era before air-conditioning. Bound by duties in Washington, D.C., Roosevelt sent this letter dated July 11, 1890, to his young son, Theodore Roosevelt, Jr., who was summering at Sagamore Hill. The illustrated letter was to be shown and read aloud to his three-year-old boy, who could not yet read.

United States
Civil Service Commission,
Washington, D. C.

July 11th '90

Blessed Ted-ped, I send you a picture letter because you are not old enough yet to read writing. Will you be glad to see your papa when he comes back? Do you want to go and play in the barn with him? and go in swimming on the beach when it is warm?

Your loving
Father

A pony and a cow go out to see the world

They meet a bear and are much frightened

He chases them back just as hard as they can run

and when they get home in safety they make up their minds they will never run away again

"THE MOST FAMOUS POSTER IN THE WORLD"

Originally published as the cover for the July 6, 1916, issue of *Leslie's Weekly* with the title "What Are You Doing for Preparedness?" this portrait of "Uncle Sam" went on to become—according to its creator, James Montgomery Flagg—"the most famous poster in the world." Over four million copies were printed between 1917 and 1918, as the United States entered World War I and began sending troops and matériel into war zones.

Flagg (1877–1960) contributed forty-six works to support the war effort. He was a member of the first Civilian Preparedness Committee organized in New York in 1917 and chaired by Grosvenor Clarkson. He also served as a member of Charles Dana Gibson's Committee of Pictorial Publicity, which was organized under the federal government's Committee on Public Information, headed by George Creel.

Because of its overwhelming popularity, the image was later adapted for use in World War II. Upon presenting President Franklin Delano Roosevelt a copy of the poster, Flagg remarked that he had been his own model for Uncle Sam to save the modeling fee. Roosevelt was impressed and replied: "I congratulate you on your resourcefulness in saving model hire. Your method suggests Yankee forebears."

Uncle Sam is one of the most popular personifications of the United States. However, the term "Uncle Sam" is of somewhat obscure derivation. Historical sources attribute the name to a meat packer who supplied meat to the army during the War of 1812—Samuel (Uncle Sam) Wilson (1766–1854). "Uncle Sam" Wilson was a man of great fairness, reliability, and honesty, who was devoted to his country—qualities now associated with "our" Uncle Sam.

DOCUMENTING THE "FORGOTTEN" PEOPLE

When they met in November 1934, photographer Dorothea Lange (1895–1965) and economist Paul Taylor (1895–1984) made a formidable team of advocates for improving living conditions of migrant laborers. Their illustrated reports provided clear accounts of the systemic causes of the problems and the need for governmental response. Lange herself selected, cropped, printed, mounted, and captioned the photographs in the reports. Her captions incorporate the very words of the people pictured, telling their own stories.

Armed with these forceful reports, H. E. Drobish, director of California's Rural Rehabilitation Office of the Emergency Relief Administration, stated in his request for federal funding to build housing camps for workers: "These laborers stand at the foot of the socioeconomic scale in our state. . . . These are the 'forgotten men, women, and children' of rural California but on these people the crops of California depend."

Between 1935 and 1943, Lange and other top-caliber photographers hired by Roy Stryker of the Resettlement Administration produced what was to become the world's best-known photographic survey, the Farm Security Administration (FSA) collection. These report albums came to the Library of Congress as part of that collection when it was transferred from the FSA in the 1940s.

On these workers the crops of California depend.

Brushing tomato plants near Indio.
March 1 - 1935

More Oklahomans reach Calif. via the cotton fields of Ariz.

"We got blowed out
in Oklahoma."

Share-cropper family
near Bakersfield
Apr. 7 - 1935

DR. FAUSTUS
O. WELLES   # 1060

White Coble cord
for hat - dyed

PLATE: 3 PLAY: Dr. Faustus
ACT: SCENE:
CHARACTER: Cardinal
DR:
APPROVED:
PRODUCTION CONTROL:
PROJECT SUPERVISOR:
DIRECTOR:
WORKSHOP:
PROJECT: 891 NAME: W.O. #:
DESIGNER: O Welles TECHNICIAN:
painted

CARDINAL

ORSON WELLES REVOLUTIONIZES THEATER

Orson Welles (1915–1985) was only twenty-two when he directed, designed costumes for, and appeared in the title role of *The Tragical History of Doctor Faustus*. This 1937 Federal Theatre Project (FTP) production of Christopher Marlowe's rarely staged Elizabethan play was, artistically, one of the most notable productions in the history of the American theater. Welles's highly innovative use of costumes, lighting, and a series of trapdoors resulted in a production in which the sense of black magic and damnation was all-pervasive.

Although the set design was very simple, the production was given intense visual effect through powerfully dramatic lighting and splendid costume coloring. The cardinal's vivid costume with its luxurious folds was designed to stand out against an essentially black thrust stage that was punctuated from the sides and above with a complex arrangement of lights.

Doctor Faustus is thought to be the only instance in which Welles designed costumes for the theater. It is also an early instance of racially integrated casting. Jack Carter, whose elegant and austere Mephistopheles contrasted mightily with the explosive Faustus of Welles, had appeared as Macbeth in the 1936 all-black production of Shakespeare's play, often known as the "Voodoo *Macbeth*" (also directed by Welles for the FTP in New York City).

Established in the administration of President Franklin Delano Roosevelt, the Federal Theatre Project was part of the Works Progress Administration and was active from 1935 to 1939. It was administered entirely by, and was wholly a function of, the federal government and was intended to provide employment for theater professionals during the Great Depression. FTP productions included plays, musical revues, vaudeville, dance, children's theater, puppetry, and circus performance. There were also black theater, and Yiddish, French, German, Italian, and Spanish language presentations. There has been nothing comparable to it since.

The Library's Federal Theatre Project Archives consist of a wide variety of materials documenting the stage productions actually mounted or considered by FTP companies. The archives include scripts, often elaborately marked to function as production guides, costume and set designs, posters, photographs, playbills, and publicity materials.

GOD BLESS AMERICA

America's unofficial national anthem was composed by an immigrant who left his home in Siberia for America when he was only five years old. The original version of "God Bless America" was written by Irving Berlin (1888–1989) during the summer of 1918 at Camp Upton, located in Yaphank, Long Island, for his Ziegfeld-style revue, *Yip, Yip, Yaphank*. "Make her victorious on land and foam, God Bless America . . ." ran the original lyric. However, Berlin decided that the solemn tone of "God Bless America" was somewhat out of keeping with the more comedic elements of the show and the song was laid aside.

In the fall of 1938, as war was again threatening Europe, Berlin decided to write a "peace" song. He recalled his "God Bless America" from twenty years earlier and made some alterations to reflect the different state of the world. Singer Kate Smith introduced the revised "God Bless America" during her radio broadcast on Armistice Day, 1938. The song was an immediate sensation; the sheet music was in great demand. Berlin soon established the God Bless America Fund, dedicating the royalties to the Boy and Girl Scouts of America.

Berlin's file of manuscripts and lyric sheets for this quintessentially American song includes manuscripts in the hand of Berlin's longtime musical secretary, Helmy Kresa (Berlin himself did not read and write music), as well as lyric sheets, and corrected proof copies for the sheet music. These materials document not only the speed with which Berlin revised this song, but also his attention to detail. The first proof copy is dated October 31, 1938; the earliest "final" version of the song is a manuscript dated November 2; and Kate Smith's historic broadcast took place on November 11. These documents show the song's step-by-step evolution from the original version of 1918 to the tune we now know.

These manuscripts are part of the Irving Berlin Collection, a remarkable collection that includes Berlin's personal papers as well as the records of the Irving Berlin Music Corp. It was presented to the Library of Congress in 1992 by Berlin's daughters, Mary Ellin Barrett, Linda Louise Emmet, and Elizabeth Irving Peters.

"WE INTERRUPT THIS BROADCAST . . ."

In addition to holding the most extensive radio broadcast collection in the country (nearly three-quarters of a million recordings), the Library of Congress offers researchers unparalleled print documentation of the medium. The NBC Radio Collection at the Library includes hundreds of thousands of scripts, business correspondence, bound press releases, and programming documentation.

This annotated script of a December 7, 1941, news report on the bombing of Pearl Harbor includes the announcer's markings for emphasis. The NBC "program analysis" index card outlines all of the network's news broadcasts of that day, including the break in regularly scheduled programming to announce the tragic news from Pearl Harbor. Other NBC documentation now at the Library outlines nearly every program heard over the network throughout World War II, including the debates that preceded our entry into the war. Described in detail, for example, are programs aired in 1941 devoted to the Fight for Freedom Committee, which promoted intervention and aid to Britain, as well as programs devoted to the isolationist America First Committee. Recordings of more than half of these programs are also in the collections of the Motion Picture, Broadcasting and Recorded Sound Division. The Library's radio collections provide not only the means to monitor the progress of World War II as experienced on the home front, but, through the extensive Armed Forces Radio and Television Service Collection, to hear American entertainment and information as heard by the fighting American forces abroad.

The microphone pictured was used by Joseph Nathan Kane to broadcast his *Famous First Facts* radio series of 1938.

В результате обмена мнений в Москве, имевшего место
12 августа с.г. я установил, что премьер министр Великобритании г.Черчилль считает невозможной организацию второго
фронта в Европе в 1942 году.

Как известно, организация второго фронта в Европе в
1942 году была предрешена во время посещения Молотовым Лон-
дона и она была отражена в согласованном англо-советском
коммюнике, опубликованном 12 июня с.г.

Известно также, что организация второго фронта в Европе имела своей целью отвлечение немецких сил с Восточного
фронта на запад, создание на западе серьезной базы сопротив-
ления немецко-фашистским силам и облегчение таким образом
положения советских войск на Советско-германском фронте в
1942 году.

Вполне понятно, что Советское Командование строило
план своих летних и осенних операций в расчете на создание
второго фронта в Европе в 1942 году.

Легко понять, что отказ правительства Великобритании от
создания второго фронта в 1942 году в Европе наносит мораль-
ный удар всей советской общественности, рассчитывающей на
создание второго фронта, осложняет положение Красной Армии
на фронте и наносит ущерб планам Советского Командования.

Я уже не говорю о том, что затруднения для Красной
Армии, создающиеся в результате отказа от создания второго
фронта в 1942 году, несомненно должны будут ухудшить военное

MEMO FROM JOSEPH STALIN

In August 1942 President Franklin Delano Roosevelt appointed W. Averell Harriman (1891–1986), head of the American Lend-Lease Program, to represent the United States at a conference with British Prime Minister Winston Churchill and Soviet Premier Joseph Stalin. The Moscow conference sought a common understanding of Soviet and Anglo-American military plans in the war against Hitler's Germany and was the highest level meeting to that time of the three allies. At the conference Churchill delivered some unwelcome news. He told Stalin that Western military planners had concluded that an Anglo-American invasion of Europe that year was military folly. The Soviets, however, desperately wanted a "second front" to relieve Nazi pressure. (By that time German forces had taken much of the western Soviet Union and held Leningrad under siege.)

положение Англии и всех остальных союзников.

Мне и моим коллегам кажется, что 1942 год представляет наиболее благоприятные условия для создания второго фронта в Европе, так как почти все силы немецких войск и притом лучшие силы отвлечены на восточный фронт, а в Европе оставлено незначительное количество сил и притом худших сил. Неизвестно будет ли представлять 1943 год такие же благоприятные условия для создания второго фронта как 1942 год. Мы считаем поэтому, что именно в 1942 году возможно и следует создать второй фронт в Европе. Но мне к сожалению не удалось убедить в этом господина премьер-министра Великобритании, а г.Гарриман представитель президента США при переговорах в Москве целиком поддержал господина премьер-министра.

И. Сталин.

13 августа 1942.

In response to Churchill's announcement, Stalin gave Harriman the memo reproduced here, one of the few documents with Stalin's handwritten signature (lower right) extant in the West. In it Stalin deplored the decision and argued that British and American forces were capable of invading Europe in 1942. In an attempt to break the joint British-American stance, Stalin also worded the memo to imply that the decision was a British one. (Churchill, however, spoke for the United States as well as his own country in this decision.)

This memo illustrates the sometimes difficult nature of the American-Soviet alliance during the war. Harriman's position as head of Lend-Lease in London and, from 1943, ambassador to the Soviet Union placed him at the center of this demanding alliance. The copious memoranda, letters, cables, and personal notes in Harriman's papers make them an indispensable source of historical documentation of that relationship as well as of the Cold War diplomacy that followed.

PRESERVING A COMIC LEGEND

On the evening of October 5, 1965, Johnny Carson welcomed the comedian Groucho Marx (1890–1977) as one of his guests on *The Tonight Show*. During the next ten minutes, Groucho delivered one of the last great impromptu comic performances of his legendary career, in which the Library of Congress featured prominently in a serious way. Groucho appeared on the show to display proudly a letter he had received from then Librarian of Congress L. Quincy Mumford requesting that he deposit his papers in the Library's Manuscript Division. In the midst of a joke-filled interplay between Groucho and Johnny, hilariously interrupted by Groucho's leering exchanges with a pretty guest to his right, Groucho asks Johnny to be serious for a moment and read the Librarian's letter aloud. At the conclusion, Groucho states: "I was so pleased when I got this [letter] . . . Having not finished public school to find my letters perhaps laying next to the Gettysburg Address I thought was quite an incongruity, in addition to being extremely thrilling . . . I'm very proud of this."

Among the collection of Groucho papers in the Library are letters exchanged by Groucho over many years with famous persons in many professions, such as T. S. Eliot, Jerry Lewis, and Edward R. Murrow, which were eventually included in a 1967 book titled *The Groucho Letters*. A 16mm kinescope copy of the portion of *The Tonight Show* containing Groucho's appearance was given by NBC to the Library and is preserved in the Motion Picture, Broadcasting and Recorded Sound Division.

AT THE GOING DOWN OF THE SUN AND IN THE MORNING WE WILL REMEMBER THEM

—Laurence Binyon, "For the Fallen"

The Vietnam Veterans Memorial, originally designed as a student project by Maya Lin at Yale University's School of Architecture in 1981, has become a profound symbol that has served to unify and reconcile a nation sorely divided by a foreign entanglement. Lin envisioned a black granite wall, in the shape of a V, on which the names of the American military dead and missing would be inscribed. She hoped that "these names, seemingly infinite in number, [would] convey the sense of overwhelming numbers, while unifying these individuals into a whole." Since its unveiling in 1982, the work—popularly known as "the wall"—has become a point of reference, inspiring a new generation of American memorials. Maya Lin's drawing is one of more than fourteen hundred design competition submissions documented in the Library of Congress as part of the Papers of the Vietnam Veterans Memorial Fund.

57

☆ *Reason* ☆

The *philosophical* part of Jefferson's library, the realm of *reason*, dealt mainly with government and science. Government was the domain of moral philosophy, of duties, of the law. The United States Constitution Jefferson treated as a great intellectual construct, based on the nature of the human person and human community. His Declaration of Independence set the manner by which the Constitution should be shaped, and Lincoln's Gettysburg Address used the key statement from the Declaration ("all men are created equal") to indicate what was still lacking in the Constitution before the addition of the Thirteenth, Fourteenth, and Fifteenth Amendments. These additions harmonized the Constitution with *both* the Declaration *and* the Gettysburg Address. The body of law was a set of implicit values that could only be articulated over time, an articulation that continues into Supreme Court decisions like that on freedom of religion (the *Gobitis* case) or equality of education (the *Brown* case). The allegorical figures of Elihu Vedder present the ideas that worked their way down from the great philosophical statements of our government, through constitutional and statutory enactment, into case law and the Supreme Court decisions. All these pit Justice against Anarchy.

The realm of science was one particularly dear to the Enlightenment intellect of Jefferson. His own house was scientifically constructed, and it contained many inventions of his own or others' devising. His "polygraph" copier was the ancestor to many recording devices. Another science that took up much of his attention was cartography, the mind's ordering of evidence about the shape and dimension of the world we live in. The patents, models, and plans for scientific tools that give us mastery over nature were at the very heart of American promise being shaped in the mind of Jefferson.

G. WILLS

BUILDING THE AMERICAN LEGAL TRADITION

The Book of the General Laws of the Inhabitants of the Jurisdiction of New-Plimouth is one of the oldest items in the Library's collection of American laws. This 1685 book reproduces the contents of a 1671 volume, which was the first edition of the laws to be printed, and adds laws enacted between 1671 and 1684. The Colony of New Plymouth, founded by the Pilgrims who arrived in the *Mayflower* in December 1620, occupied the southeastern corner of the present state of Massachusetts. It was soon surpassed in population and wealth by the Massachusetts Bay Colony, centered on Boston, and was annexed to Massachusetts in 1691.

The Colony of New Plymouth made several major contributions to American legal institutions. In 1636, when the population was less than three thousand people, a committee of the General Court composed a legal code, the first produced in North America. It contains what one scholar has called a "rudimentary bill of rights," which guarantees trial by jury and stipulates that all laws are to be made with the consent of the freemen of the colony. The "General Fundamentals" of the 1671 code state that "no person . . . shall be endamaged in respect of life, limb, liberty, good name or estate . . . but by virtue of some express law of the General Court of this Colony, the known Law of God, or the good and equitable laws of our Nation."

The punishment for adultery set out in this code and in the 1694 laws of the Massachusetts Bay Colony, stipulating that adulterers must bear the letters "A" and "D," provides the basis for some of the best-known elements in Nathaniel Hawthorne's 1850 novel *The Scarlet Letter*.

John Beauchamp on the other part; being thereunto deputed by the said Merchants, and the rest Adventuring as aforesaid; as appeareth by a Deed, bearing Date *Nov. 6th* in the third Year of the Reign of our Soveraign Lord *Charles*, by the Grace of God King of *England, Scotland, France* and *Ireland, &c.* Anno Dom. 1627.   Be it Known therefore unto all Men by these presents, that according to our first intents, for the better effecting the glory of God, the enlargement of the Dominions of our said Soveraign Lord the King, and the special good of His Subjects; by virtue as well of our Combination aforesaid, as also the several Graunts by us procured in the Names of *John Peirce* and *William Bradford*, their Heirs, and Associates; together with our lawful Right, in respect of Vacancy, Donation or Purchase of the Natives, and our full Purchase of the Adventurers before expressed, have given unto, Allotted, Assigned and Granted to all and every person or persons, whose Name or Names shall follow upon this publick Record, such proportion or proportions of Grounds, with all and singular the priviledges thereto belonging, as aforesaid, to him or them, his or their Heirs, and Assigns successively for ever; to be Holden of His Majesty of *England*, His Heirs and Successors, as of His Mannor of *East-Greenwich*, in the County of *Kent*; in free and common Soccage, and not in Capite, nor by Knights Service; yielding and paying to our said Soveraign Lord the King, His Heirs and Successors for ever, one fifth part of the Oar of the Mines of Gold and Silver; and one other fifth part to the President and Council, which shall be had, possessed and obtained as aforesaid. And whatsoever Lands are or shall be granted to any the said *William Bradford, Edward Winslow, William Brewster, Isaac Allerton,* their Heirs or Associates as aforesaid; being acknowledged in publick Court, and brought to the publick Records of the several Inheritances of the Subjects of our Soveraign Lord the King, within this Government; it shall be lawful for the Governour of *New-Plimouth* aforesaid, from time to time successively, to give under the common Seal of the Government a Coppy of the said Graunt so Recorded; Confirming the said Lands to him or them, his or their Heirs and Assigns for ever; with the several Bounds and Limits of the same, which shall be sufficient Evidence in Law from time to time, and at all times, for the said party or parties, his or their Heirs or Assigns; to Have and to Hold the said portion of Land so Granted, Bounded and Recorded as aforesaid; with all and singular the Appurtenances thereunto belonging, to the only proper use and behoof of the said party or parties, his or their Heirs and Assigns for ever.

And their far-ther Right in respect of Va-cancy, Dona-tion & Pur-chase of the Natives, to Give and Graunt Lands, &c.

CHAP

The Copy being Imperfect most of these Errata's following happened thereby.

PAge 3 of the Preface, Line 14. Read acquire. p 2 of the Book l. 29. for wars. r. war, p 3. l. 21. because &c. begins the second Section l. 36 r Recorder: p 6 l.21. r. Sureties. p 7. l.46. r. fifth. p. 10. l.25. r. willsully. l.37. r. 28. p. 17. l.42. r. 28 p.20. l.39. r. each. p.21. l.4. r. each. p. 23. l.19. r. filth. p.26. l.16. die ing. p. 27 l. 17. add the. p. 28 Title *Dures* p. 30. l.16. r. County. p. 31. l.4. r. Country. l.40. r. Country. l.42. r. Country. p. 33. l 9 r. if. l. 25. r. as l.44 r. or. p. 34 l. 11. r. stature. l. 17. r. stature. p.36. l. 18. r. subject. p. 39. l. 15. r. Mare. l.15. r. hitherto. p.44. l.32. r. ac-crued. l.6. r. sue. l.11. r. of p. 48. l. 37. r. if. p.50. l.24. r pious. p. 54. l.20. r hundred. p.66. l. 19. r Town p.d. l 35. r if. p.51. l. 18. after Swear dele 3. the same &c. follows in the second Section. l.32 r. signed and. p 69 l. 19. r the plantations p.71. l. 8. r. make. p.72. l.15. r Ward. p.74. l. 38. dele with. p.75. l.2. r. Share Atts ched the Goods or Lands of said A.B. to sufficient value, and Last Summer at this House or place of usual Abode, &c.

CHAP. I.

The General

Fundamentals.

Anno. 1636. and Revised 1671.

1.   WEE the Associates of the Colony of New-Plimouth, coming hither as free born Subjects of the Kingdome of England, Endued with all and singular the Priviledges belonging to such: Being Assembled,

Do Enact, Ordain and Constitute; that no Act, Imposition, Law or Ordinance be Made or Imposed upon us at present or to come, but such as shall be Enacted by consent of the body of Freemen or Associates, or their Representatives legally assembled; which is according to the free Liberties of the free born People of *England*.

Laws to be made by the Freemen or their represen-tatives.

2. And for the well Governing this Colony: It is also Resolved and Ordered, that there be a free Election annually, of Governour, Deputy Go-vernour and Assistants, by the Vote of the Freemen of this Corporation.

Annually cho-sen by the free men.

3. It is also Enacted, that Justice and Right be equally and impartially Administred unto all, not sold, denied or causelesly deterred unto any.

Justice to be equally and speedily admi-nistred.

4. It is also Enacted, that no person in this Government shall suffer or be indamaged, in respect of Life, Limb, Liberty, Good Name or Estate, under colour of Law, or countenance of Authority, but by Virtue or Equity of some express Law of the General Court of this Colony, or the good and equitable Laws of our Nation, suitable for us, in matters which are of a civil nature (as by the Court here hath been accustomed) wherein we have no particular Law of our own. And that none shall suffer as aforesaid, without being brought to answer by due course and process of Law.

None to suffer but according to Law, and by due course & pro-cess of Law.

5. And that all Cases, whither Capital, Criminal, or between man and man,

B 2

LAYING THE GROUNDWORK FOR THE DECLARATION OF INDEPENDENCE

The Virginia Declaration of Rights was written in May 1776 by George Mason (1725–1792) and Thomas Ludwell Lee (c. 1730–1777) as a call to action by the Virginia Convention meeting in Williamsburg. It was published in the *Pennsylvania Evening Post* on June 6, and was unanimously adopted by the Virginia Convention on June 12. Thomas Jefferson may have received a copy directly from Mason and Lee, his fellow Virginia planters and revolutionaries. In any event, he drew extensively from the Declaration of Rights, as well as from his own drafts of a new constitution for Virginia, when composing the Declaration of Independence in June 1776. For example, the Virginia Declaration of Rights proposes:

of such laws, are generally dangerous, and ought to be avoided.

N.B. It is proposed to make some alteration in this last article when reported to the house. Perhaps somewhat like the following

That all laws having a retrospect to crimes, & punishing offences committed before the existence of such laws are dangerous, and ought to be avoided, except in cases of great & evident necessity, when the safety of the state absolutely requires them. — This is thought to state with more precision the doctrine respecting ex post facto laws & to signify to posterity that it is considered not so much as a law of right, as the great law of necessity, which by a well known maxim is — allowed to supersede all human institutions.

Another is agreed to in committee condemning the use of general warrants; & one other to prevent the suspension of laws, or the execution of them.

The above clauses, with some small alterations, & the addition of one or two more, have already been agreed to in the Committee appointed to prepare a declaration of rights; when this business is finished in the house, the committee will proceed to the ordinance of government.

T. L. Lee —

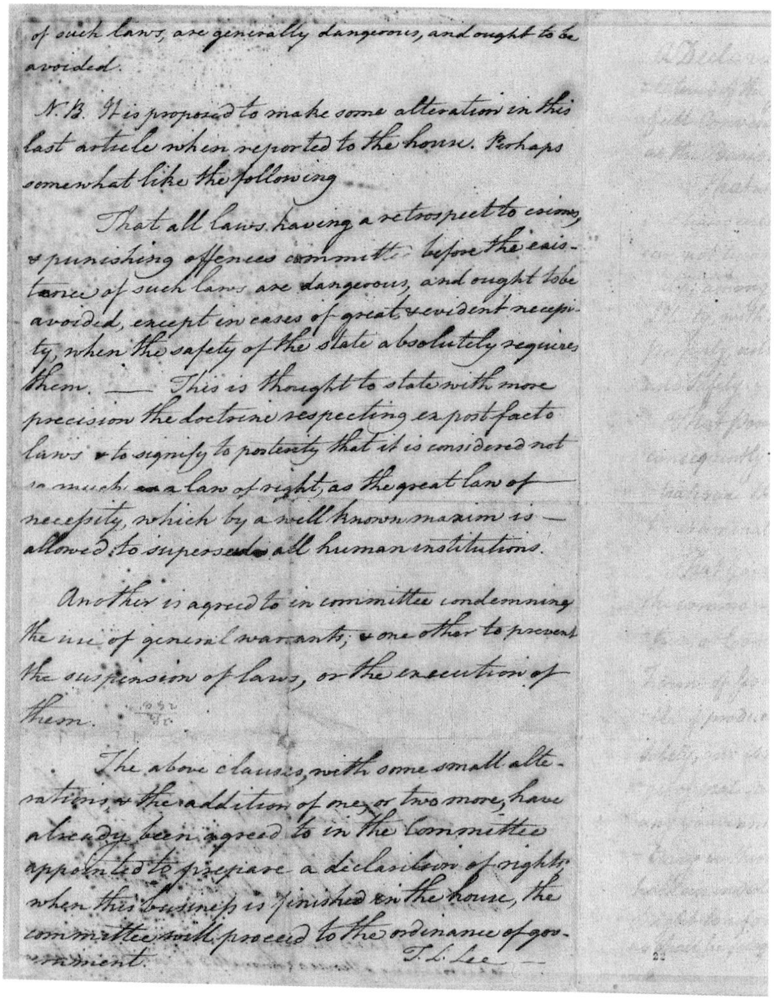

That all men are born equally free and independant [sic], *and have certain inherent natural Rights, . . . among which are the Enjoyment of Life and Liberty, with the Means of acquiring and possessing Property, and pursueing* [sic] *and obtaining Happiness and Safety.*

While the Declaration of Independence states:

. . . that all men are created equal, that they are endowed by their creator with certain unalienable rights, that among these are life, liberty, and the pursuit of happiness.

Seen here is Mason's first draft of the Declaration of Rights, to which Lee added several clauses. Their work also had a profound influence on the men who shaped the Federal Constitution and the Bill of Rights.

A Declaration by the Representatives of the UNITED STATES
OF AMERICA, in General Congress assembled.

When in the course of human events it becomes necessary for one people to
dissolve the political bands which have connected them with another, and to as-
sume among the powers of the earth the ~~separate and equal~~ station to
which the laws of nature & of nature's god entitle them, a decent respect
to the opinions of mankind requires that they should declare the causes
which impel them to the separation.

We hold these truths to be self-evident; that all men are
created equal, that they are endowed by their creator with
inherent & inalienable rights, that among these are the
life & liberty, & the pursuit of happiness; that to secure these rights, go-
-vernments are instituted among men, deriving their just powers from
the consent of the governed: that whenever any form of government
becomes destructive of these ends, it is the right of the people to alter
or to abolish it, & to institute new government, laying it's foundation on
such principles & organising it's powers in such form, as to them shall
seem most likely to effect their safety & happiness. prudence indeed
will dictate that governments long established should not be changed for
light & transient causes: and accordingly all experience hath shewn that
mankind are more disposed to suffer while evils are sufferable, than to
right themselves by abolishing the forms to which they are accustomed. but
when a long train of abuses & usurpations [begun at a distinguished period,
&] pursuing invariably the same object, evinces a design to reduce
them under absolute Despotism, it is their right, it is their duty, to throw off such
& to provide new guards for their future security. such has
been the patient sufferance of these colonies; & such is now the necessity
which constrains them to expunge their former systems of government.
the history of the present king of Great Britain is a history of unremitting injuries and
usurpations, [among which appears no solitary fact to contra-
-dict the uniform tenor of the rest all of which have in direct object the
establishment of an absolute tyranny over these states. to prove this, let facts be
submitted to a candid world, for the truth of which we pledge a faith
yet unsullied by falsehood.

64

"WE HOLD THESE TRUTHS TO BE SELF-EVIDENT . . ."

The "original Rough draught" of the Declaration of Independence, one of the great milestones in American history, shows the evolution of the text from the initial "fair copy" draft by Thomas Jefferson to the final text adopted by Congress on the morning of July 4, 1776.

On June 11, in anticipation of the impending vote for independence from Great Britain, the Continental Congress appointed five men—Thomas Jefferson, John Adams, Benjamin Franklin, Roger Sherman, and Robert Livingston—to write a declaration that would make clear to all the people why this break from their sovereign, King George III, was both necessary and inevitable.

The committee then appointed Jefferson to draft a statement. Jefferson produced a "fair" copy of his draft declaration, which became the basic text of his "original Rough draught." The text was first submitted to Adams, then Franklin, and finally to the other two members of the committee. Before the committee submitted the declaration to Congress on June 28, they made forty-seven emendations to the document. During the ensuing congressional debates of July 1–4, Congress adopted thirty-nine further revisions to the committee draft.

The first page of the four-page "Rough draught" shown here illustrates the numerous additions, deletions, and corrections made at each step along the way. Although most of these alterations are in Jefferson's own distinctive hand—he later indicated the changes he believed to have been made by Adams and Franklin—he opposed many of the revisions made to his original composition.

Late in life Jefferson endorsed this document: "Independence. Declaration of original Rough draught."

WASHINGTON'S TROOPS HEAR THE DECLARATION OF INDEPENDENCE

This is one of only twenty-four surviving copies of the first printed Declaration of Independence, created on July 4, 1776, by the Philadelphia printer John Dunlap. This copy of what is called the "Dunlap Broadside" was George Washington's personal copy, sent to him on July 6 by the president of the Continental Congress, John Hancock, whose letter is shown to the left of the broadside. General Washington had the Declaration read to his assembled troops in New York on July 9. Later that night the Americans destroyed a bronze and lead statue of King George III that stood at the foot of Broadway on the Bowling Green.

Washington's copy of the Declaration is broken at lines thirty-four and fifty-four, and the text below line fifty-four is missing; presumably the paper weakened and broke off where it was frequently folded. The Library also has a complete copy of this rare Dunlap broadside in the Broadside Collection and recently acquired a unique copy of the Declaration of Independence, printed in July 1776, in Ulster County, New York, with the Marian S. Carson Collection.

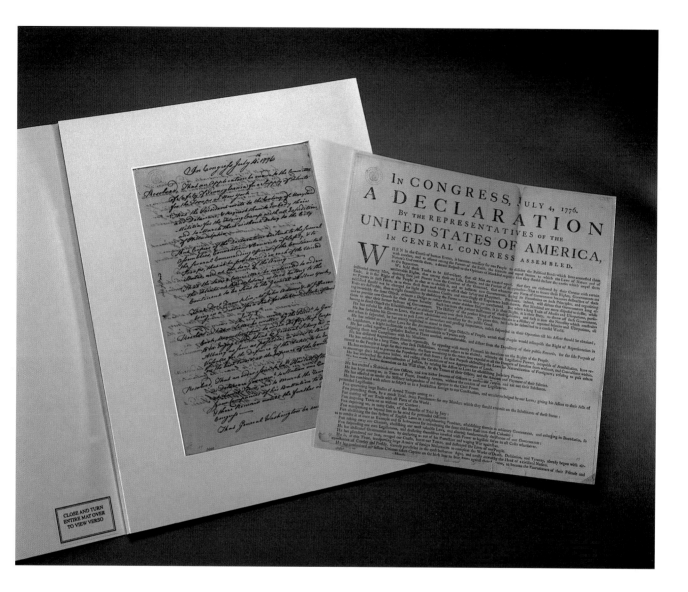

the opinions of the conftituents; a point to which no man of virtue would ever agree. By confidering the members of the houfe of commons as *fenators of the publick*, we may conceive them to be (in a certain degree) the reprefentatives and guardians of all Britifh commoners, wherefoever difperfed. It is indeed to be hoped, that fome time or other, a better mode of election may be eftablifhed to make the reprefentation more equal, but till that happens we muft abide by the prefent regulations, and fupport the dignity and authority of the houfe of commons, (the palladium of our liberties) though the method of forming it is not perfect.

REFLEC-

In what Degree?

Who are Britifh commoners? Are the American Colonists such?

x why, don't you fet about it?

REFLECTIONS

MORAL and POLITICAL.

PART I.

AMONG all the errors to which mankind is fubject, none are more dangerous than thofe which arife from excellencies or virtues *mifunderftood*. As furely as an exceffive generofity will deftroy a great fortune, or an extream frugality will annihilate the enjoyment of riches, fo furely will an unlimited exercife of liberty deftroy that *reafonable liberty*, which is alone confiftent with *fociety*.

B

In

THOMAS JEFFERSON'S LIBRARY

Thomas Jefferson had a passion for books and assembled the finest private library in America. From the Philadelphia book dealer N. G. Dufief, Jefferson acquired several books from the late Benjamin Franklin's personal collection, including two pamphlets, bound together, about taxation of the colonies: *Reflections moral and political on Great Britain and her colonies* by Matthew Wheelock, and *Thoughts on the origin and nature of government* by Allan Ramsay. As Jefferson wrote to Dufief, he was especially pleased to receive "the precious reliques of Doctor Franklin," which he valued "not only [for] the intrinsic value of whatever came from him, but [also] my particular affection for him." Franklin had written lengthy and heated notes in the margins of the pamphlets on nearly every page, beginning in the preface to the first pamphlet (seen opposite) where Franklin, reading of the author's hope that "a better mode of election may be established to make the representation more equal," impatiently interjects "why don't you get about it?"

When the British burned the Capitol during the War of 1812, Congress lost its entire book collection in the flames. Jefferson proposed to sell to Congress his own private library, which consisted of over six thousand volumes including legal tomes, maps and charts, ancient and modern history, some belles lettres, and the seminal works of such political philosophers as John Locke and Montesquieu, who had inspired the Founding Fathers and shaped their political thought. While some members of Congress objected to the notion of purchasing so many books not directly related to the business of legislating, Jefferson convinced the majority that "there is, in fact, no subject to which a Member of Congress might not have occasion to refer." So it is that the Library of Congress has grown from the seed of Jefferson's own library, universal in subject matter and format, into a library that serves as Congress's working research collection, as well as a symbol of the central role that free and unfettered access to information plays in our modern democracy.

LAWS GOVERNING SLAVERY

Slavery in the United States was governed by an extensive body of law developed from the 1660s to the 1860s. Every slave state had its own slave code and body of court decisions. All slave codes made slavery a permanent condition, inherited through the mother, and defined slaves as property, usually in the same terms as those applied to real estate. Slaves, being property, could not own property or be a party to a contract. Since marriage is a form of contract, no slave marriage had any legal standing. All codes also had sections regulating free blacks, who were still subject to controls on their movements and employment and were often required to leave the state after emancipation.

When the District of Columbia was established in 1800, the laws of Maryland, including its slave laws, remained in force. Additional laws on slavery and free blacks were then made by the District, and by Southern standards its slave codes were moderate. Slaves were permitted to hire out their services and to live apart from their masters. Free blacks were permitted to live in the city and to operate private schools. By 1860 the District of Columbia was home to 11,131 free blacks and 3,185 slaves.

The manuscript volume shown with the published slave code is arranged by topic, listing relevant sections of Maryland and District of Columbia laws as well as the applicable court decisions. It is almost certainly a "practice book," produced within a law firm for the use of its attorneys and clerks, who could refer to it when drafting contracts and legal briefs. That such a book exists indicates something of the volume and routine character of legal work surrounding transactions in human property.

Slavery in the District of Columbia ended on April 16, 1862, when President Lincoln signed a law that provided for compensation to slave owners. An Emancipation Claims Commission hired a Baltimore slave trader to assess the value of each freed slave, and awarded compensation for 2,989 slaves. The printed slavery code exhibited here was published on March 17, 1862, just one month before slavery in the District ended and the laws became of historical interest only.

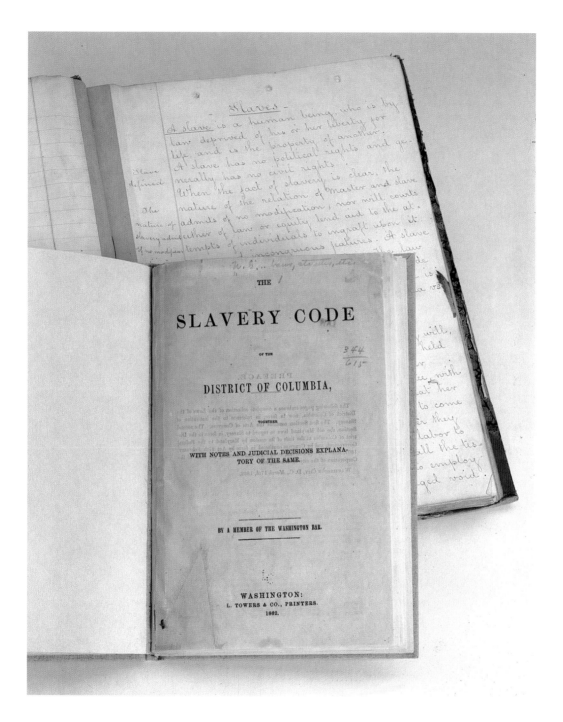

- Slaves -

A slave is a human being, who is by
law deprived of his or her liberty for
life, and is the property of another.
A slave has no political rights and generally has no civil rights.
When the fact of slavery is clear, the
nature of the relation of master and slave
admits of no modification; nor will courts
either of law or equity lend aid to the attempts of individuals to ingraft upon it
incongruous features.

*Slave
defined*

*The
nature of
slavery admits
of no modifica-*

THE

SLAVERY CODE

OF THE

DISTRICT OF COLUMBIA,

TOGETHER

WITH NOTES AND JUDICIAL DECISIONS EXPLANA-
TORY OF THE SAME.

BY A MEMBER OF THE WASHINGTON BAR.

WASHINGTON:
L. TOWERS & CO., PRINTERS.
1862.

In pursuance of the sixth section of the act of congress entitled "An act to suppress insurrection and to punish treason and rebellion, to seize and confiscate property of rebels, and for other purposes" Approved July 17. 1862, and which act, and the Joint Resolution explanatory thereof, are herewith published, I, Abraham Lincoln, President of the United States, do hereby proclaim to, and warn all persons within the contemplation of said sixth section to cease participating in, aiding, countenancing, or abetting the existing rebellion, or any rebellion against the government of the United States, and to return to their proper allegiance to the United States, on pain of the forfeitures and seizures, as within and by said sixth section provided—

And I hereby make known that it is my purpose, upon the next meeting of Congress, to again recommend the adoption of a practical measure for tendering pecuniary aid to the free choice or rejection, of any and all States, which may then be recognizing and practically sustaining the authority of the United States, and which may then have voluntarily adopted, or thereafter may voluntarily adopt, gradual abolishment of slavery within such State or States— that the object is to practically restore, thenceforward to be maintain, the constitutional relation between the general government, and each, and all the States, wherein that relation

17232

EMANCIPATION

Abraham Lincoln shared this first draft of his Emancipation Proclamation with his cabinet on July 22, 1862. The reaction of the men present was mixed. Secretary of War Edwin Stanton saw the move as a military measure designed to deprive the Confederacy of slave labor through disaffection and desertion. It would also render freedmen eligible to serve in the Union army. Stanton advocated the proclamation's immediate release. Treasury Secretary Salmon Chase also supported immediate emancipation. Others argued that such a move would cost the president the upcoming elections, as "there is no sentiment in the North, even among extreme men which now is now suspended, or disturbed; and that, for this object, the war, as it has been, will be, prosecuted. And, as a fit and necessary military measure for effecting this object, I, as Commander-in-Chief of the Army and Navy of the United States, do order and declare that on the first day of January in the year of our Lord one thousand, eight hundred and sixty three, all persons held as slaves within any State or states, wherein the constitutional authority of the United States, shall not then be practically recognized, submitted to, and maintained, shall then, thenceforward, and forever, be free,

17233

demands the proposed measure." Nevertheless, Lincoln set January 1, 1863, as the deadline for states in rebellion to return to the Union. Upon that date, as "a fit and necessary military measure," he would "order and declare [that] . . . all persons held as slaves within any state or states, wherein the constitutional authority of the United States shall not be practically recognized, submitted to, and maintained, shall then, thenceforward, and forever be free."

Acting largely on his own, Lincoln subsequently rewrote the draft proclamation, and on September 22 issued what is known as the Preliminary Emancipation Proclamation. He issued the final proclamation on January 1, 1863.

DRAFTING THE GETTYSBURG ADDRESS

Seen here are the earliest two of five known drafts in Abraham Lincoln's handwriting of what may be the most famous American speech. Delivered in Gettysburg, Pennsylvania, at the dedication of the National Cemetery on November 19, 1863, it is now familiarly known as "The Gettysburg Address." In writing the speech, Lincoln drew inspiration from his favorite historical document, the Declaration of Independence, and equated the catastrophic suffering caused by the Civil War with the efforts of the American people to create a republic founded on the proposition that "all men are created equal."

Details of the composition of the Gettysburg Address remain uncertain. The draft at left, presumed to be the only working, or predelivery, draft, is commonly called the "Nicolay Copy" because it was owned by John Nicolay, Lincoln's private secretary. The first page of the Nicolay Copy is on White House (then Executive Mansion) stationery, lending strong support to the theory that it was drafted in Washington, D.C. But the second page is on different paper, suggesting that Lincoln rewrote the final paragraph of the address in Gettysburg on November 18

74

Four score and seven years ago our fathers brought forth, upon this continent, a new nation, conceived in Liberty, and dedicated to the proposition that all men are created equal.

Now we are engaged in a great civil war, testing whether that nation, or any nation, so conceived, and so dedicated, can long endure. We are met here on a great battle-field of that war. We have come to dedicate a portion of it, as the final resting place for those who here gave their lives that that nation might live. It is altogether fitting and proper that we should do this.

But in a larger sense we can not dedicate— we can not consecrate— we can not hallow this ground. The brave men, living and dead, who struggled here, have consecrated it far above our poor power to add or detract. The world will little note, nor long remember, what we say here, but can never forget what they did here. It is for us, the living, rather to be dedicated here to the unfinished work, which they have, thus far, so nobly carried on. It is rather

for us to be here dedicated to the great task remaining before us— that from these honored dead we take increased devotion to the cause for which they here gave the last full measure of devotion— that we here highly resolve that these dead shall not have died in vain; that this nation shall have a new birth of freedom; and that this government of the people, by the people, for the people, shall not perish from the earth.

while staying at the home of Judge David Wills, who had conceived the idea of a National Cemetery and had organized the dedication ceremonies. Arguments against the Nicolay Copy's qualifying as the actual reading copy stem partly from the unnatural flow of the text from one page to the next. Further, there are discrepancies between the draft and newspaper accounts of the speech by reporters at the scene. Stories about Lincoln writing the original Address on the train en route to Gettysburg and on the back of an envelope have been totally discredited.

The second copy, at right, is known as the "Hay Copy" because it was owned by another of Lincoln's personal secretaries, John Hay. It was probably copied out after the speech was given. When Nicolay died in 1901, he left his copy of the address to Hay, a lifelong friend and associate. Hay died in 1906, and ten years later his surviving children presented the Nicolay Copy and the Hay Copy to the Library of Congress. Between the two copies there are over sixty differences in word choice, spelling, and punctuation, providing close readers unique insights into Abraham Lincoln's creative process.

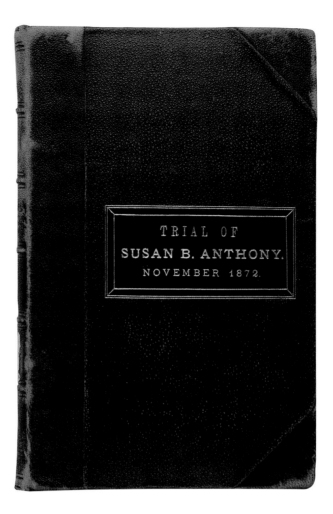

SUSAN B. ANTHONY, DEFENDANT

Susan B. Anthony's personal copy of *An Account of the Proceedings on the Trial of Susan B. Anthony* is one of nearly four hundred items from her personal library of feminist and antislavery literature that Anthony gave to the Library of Congress in 1903. Anthony (1820–1906), the noted woman suffrage crusader, was arrested and indicted on Thanksgiving Day, 1872, for having "knowingly voted without having a lawful right to vote." Citing their rights as citizens under the Fourteenth Amendment of the Constitution, Anthony, her sister Mary, and four other women had voted in the presidential election on November 5. After her arrest, Anthony proclaimed that "this government is not a democracy. It is not a republic. It is an odious aristocracy; a hateful oligarchy of sex . . . which ordains all men sovereigns, all women subjects, carries dissension, discord, and rebellion into every home of the nation." (The complete speech is the Appendix to the *Trial*.)

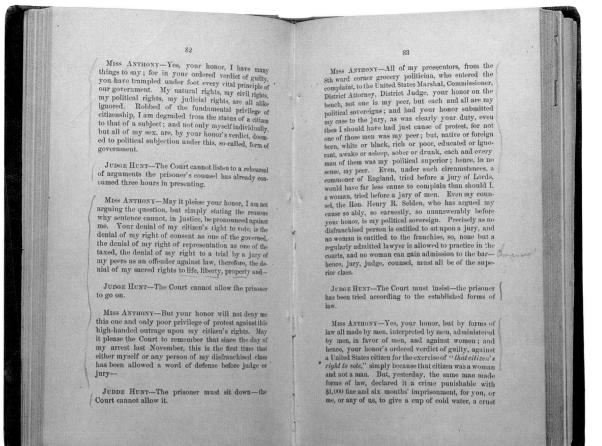

MISS ANTHONY—Yes, your honor, I have many things to say; for in your ordered verdict of guilty, you have trampled under foot every vital principle of our government. My natural rights, my civil rights, my political rights, my judicial rights, are all alike ignored. Robbed of the fundamental privilege of citizenship, I am degraded from the status of a citizen to that of a subject; and not only myself individually, but all of my sex, are, by your honor's verdict, doomed to political subjection under this, so-called, form of government.

JUDGE HUNT—The Court cannot listen to a rehearsal of arguments the prisoner's counsel has already consumed three hours in presenting.

MISS ANTHONY—May it please your honor, I am not arguing the question, but simply stating the reasons why sentence cannot, in justice, be pronounced against me. Your denial of my citizen's right to vote, is the denial of my right of consent as one of the governed, the denial of my right of representation as one of the taxed, the denial of my right to a trial by a jury of my peers as an offender against law, therefore, the denial of my sacred rights to life, liberty, property and—

JUDGE HUNT—The Court cannot allow the prisoner to go on.

MISS ANTHONY—But your honor will not deny me this one and only poor privilege of protest against this high-handed outrage upon my citizen's rights. May it please the Court to remember that since the day of my arrest last November, this is the first time that either myself or any person of my disfranchised class has been allowed a word of defense before judge or jury—

JUDGE HUNT—The prisoner must sit down—the Court cannot allow it.

MISS ANTHONY—All of my prosecutors, from the 8th ward corner grocery politician, who entered the complaint, to the United States Marshal, Commissioner, District Attorney, District Judge, your honor on the bench, not one is my peer, but each and all are my political sovereigns; and had your honor submitted my case to the jury, as was clearly your duty, even then I should have had just cause of protest, for not one of those men was my peer; but, native or foreign born, white or black, rich or poor, educated or ignorant, awake or asleep, sober or drunk, each and every man of them was my political superior; hence, in no sense, my peer. Even, under such circumstances, a commoner of England, tried before a jury of Lords, would have far less cause to complain than should I, a woman, tried before a jury of men. Even my counsel, the Hon. Henry R. Selden, who has argued my cause so ably, so earnestly, so unanswerably before your honor, is my political sovereign. Precisely as no disfranchised person is entitled to sit upon a jury, and no woman is entitled to the franchise, so, none but a regularly admitted lawyer is allowed to practice in the courts, and no woman can gain admission to the bar— hence, jury, judge, counsel, must all be of the superior class.

JUDGE HUNT—The Court must insist—the prisoner has been tried according to the established forms of law.

MISS ANTHONY—Yes, your honor, but by forms of law all made by men, interpreted by men, administered by men, in favor of men, and against women; and hence, your honor's ordered verdict of guilty, against a United States citizen for the exercise of "*that citizen's right to vote*," simply because that citizen was a woman and not a man. But, yesterday, the same man made forms of law, declared it a crime punishable with $1,000 fine and six months' imprisonment, for you, or me, or any of us, to give a cup of cold water, a crust

At the trial, the judge penned his decision before hearing the case (his first criminal case) and discharged the jury because he maintained that there were no questions of fact for them to consider. He found Anthony guilty of voting illegally, fined her $100, and then made the mistake of asking her if she had anything to say.

"Yes, your honor," seethed Anthony, "I have many things to say; for in your ordered verdict of guilty, you have trampled under foot every vital principle of our government. My natural rights, my civil rights, my political rights, my judicial rights, are all alike ignored. Robbed of the fundamental privilege of citizenship, I am degraded from the status of a citizen to that of a subject; and not only myself individually, but all of my sex, are, by your honor's verdict, doomed to political subjection under this, so-called, form of government."

Anthony's copy of the *Trial* is inscribed by her as a gift to the Library and has a number of items tipped in after the text, including Anthony's petition to Congress seeking remission of the fine and the congressional committee report denying her request.

THE ART OF GOVERNMENT

The Library of Congress had outgrown its quarters in the Capitol by 1886, when Congress authorized the building of a separate edifice to house its collections. Congress aspired to build an imposing and beautiful public building, one as grand as any single library in Europe, one that would reflect the young nation's dreams and ambitions and embody America's native optimism about the ability of this nation to build its future on the solid foundation of the written traditions of the great ancient civilizations. That building, completed in 1897, is now known as the Thomas Jefferson Building.

Elihu Vedder (1836–1923), a prominent easel and mural painter who was born in New York but lived in Rome, was commissioned in January 1895 to prepare five mural panels for the new building then under construction. Vedder chose to address the theme of "Government," and sketches for two of the five panels on that subject are shown here: "Anarchy," which, it is clear from the arrangement of the panels in the building, springs from "Corrupt Legislation"; and "Peace and Prosperity," the offspring of "Good Administration." "Anarchy" features a wild, naked female figure brandishing a wine glass and a burning scroll. She is trampling the products of civilized society and is supported by figures and emblems representing Violence and Ignorance. In "Peace and Prosperity," all is calm, as a serene nude female figure symbolizing peace offers laurel wreaths to flanking youths representing the Arts on the one hand, and Agriculture on the other.

A MATTER OF RELIGIOUS PRINCIPLE

"I do not salute the flag because I have promised to do the will of God," wrote ten-year-old Billy Gobitas to the board of the Minersville (Pennsylvania) School District in 1935. His refusal, and that of his sister Lillian (age twelve), touched off one of several constitutional legal cases delineating the tension between the authority of the state to require respect for national symbols and the right of individuals to freedom of speech.

The Gobitas children attended a public school, which, as did most public schools at that time, required students to salute and pledge allegiance to the flag of the United States. The Gobitas children were members of the Jehovah's Witnesses, a church that in 1935 concluded that the ceremonial saluting of a national flag was a form of idolatry, a violation of the commandment in Exodus 20:4–6 that "thou shalt not make unto thee any graven image, nor bow down to them . . ." and forbidden as well by John 5:21 and Matthew 22:21. On October 22, 1935, Billy Gobitas acted on this belief and refused to participate in the daily flag-and-pledge ceremony. The next day Lillian Gobitas did the same. In this letter Billy Gobitas in his own hand explained his reasons to the school board. On November 6, 1935, the directors of the Minersville School District voted to expel the two for insubordination.

The Watchtower Society of the Jehovah's Witnesses sued on behalf of the children. The decisions of the U.S. district court and court of appeals were in favor of the children. But in 1940 the U.S. Supreme Court by an eight to one vote reversed these lower court decisions and ruled that the government had inherent authority to compel respect for the flag as a central symbol of national unity. *Minersville School District v. Gobitis* (a printer's error has enshrined a misspelling of the Gobitas name in constitutional case law) was not, however, the last legal word on the subject. In 1943 the Supreme Court by a six to three vote in the case of *West Virginia State Board of Education v. Barnette* reconsidered its decision in *Gobitis* and held that the right of free speech guaranteed in the First Amendment to the Constitution denies the government the authority to compel the saluting of the American flag or the recitation of the Pledge of Allegiance.

Minersville, Pa.
Nov. 5, 1935

Our School Directors

Dear Sirs

I do not salute the flag because I have promised to do the will of God. That means that I must not worship anything out of harmony with God's law. In the twentieth chapter of Exodus it is stated, "Thou shalt not make unto thee any graven image, nor bow down to them nor serve them for I the Lord thy God am a jealous God visiting the iniquity of the fathers upon the children

unto the third and fourth generation of them that hate me. I am a true follower of Christ. I do not salute the flag because I do not love my country but I love my country and I love God more and I must obey His commandments.

Your Pupil,
Billy Gobitas

DECREE # 2

1. The appellees in Nos. 1, 2 and 3, the respondents in No. 4, and the petitioners in No. 5 are permanently enjoined from excluding the appellants in Nos. 1, 2 and 3, the petitioners in No. 4, and the respondents in No. 5 from any public school on the ground of race.

2. The cases are remanded to the respective federal district and state courts for appropriate decrees to carry out the mandate of this Court in the light of the decisions in Brown v. Board of Education, 347 U.S. 483, and Bolling v. Sharpe, 347 U.S. 497.

3. The rights of the appellants in Nos. 1, 2 and 3, the petitioners in No. 4, and the respondents in No. 5 must be given effect immediately where all the relevant considerations controlling a court of equity make it feasible to do so. [Provided that steps toward full compliance with the standards enunciated in Section 4, infra, are undertaken at once by the affected school districts, the admission of a named plaintiff may be delayed for a reasonable period, not to exceed one school cycle of 12 years.]

4. Insofar as reorganization may be necessary in the school districts affected by our judgment and mandate and in other school districts similarly situated, so as to make effective this decree that no student shall be denied admission to any public school because of his race, the respective lower courts are to require that any new or reorganized school districts to be established by local authorities shall be geographically compact, contiguous and non-gerrymandered. And it shall further be made incumbent upon local authorities that within a given school district Negro students be

BROWN V. BOARD OF EDUCATION

The deliberations of the Supreme Court in its landmark case of 1954, *Brown v. Board of Education of Topeka*, which found school segregation to be unconstitutional, are well documented in the Library's manuscript collections. After the *Brown* opinion was announced, the Court heard additional arguments during the following term on the decree implementing the ruling. While the NAACP lawyers had proposed to use the word "forthwith" to achieve an accelerated desegregation timetable, Chief Justice Earl Warren adopted Justice Felix Frankfurter's suggestion to use a phrase associated with the revered Oliver Wendell Holmes, "with all deliberate speed." Shortly after Warren retired from the Court he acknowledged that "all deliberate speed" was chosen as a benchmark because "there

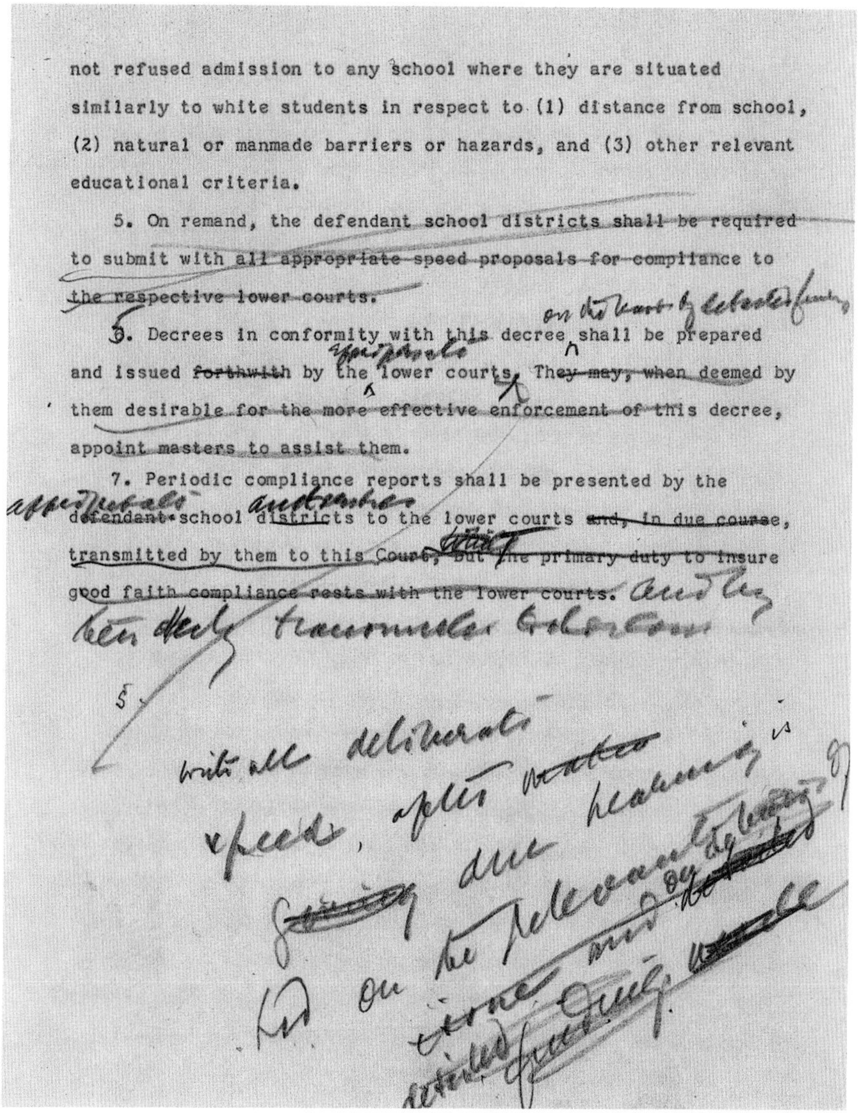

not refused admission to any school where they are situated
similarly to white students in respect to (1) distance from school,
(2) natural or manmade barriers or hazards, and (3) other relevant
educational criteria.

5. On remand, the defendant school districts shall be required
to submit with all appropriate speed proposals for compliance to
the respective lower courts.

~~5.~~ 6. Decrees in conformity with this decree shall be prepared
and issued ~~forthwith~~ by the lower courts. They may, when deemed by
them desirable for the more effective enforcement of this decree,
appoint masters to assist them.

7. Periodic compliance reports shall be presented by the
defendant school districts to the lower courts and, in due course,
transmitted by them to this Court, but the primary duty to insure
good faith compliance rests with the lower courts.

[Handwritten marginal and interlinear annotations in pencil, largely illegible, including phrases such as "with all deliberate speed, after... due hearing... on the relevant..."]

---

were so many blocks preventing an immediate solution of the thing in reality that the best we could look for would be a progression of action." It became clear over time that critics of desegregation were using the doctrine to delay compliance with *Brown*, and in 1964 Justice Hugo Black declared in a desegregation opinion that "the time for mere 'deliberate speed' has run out." This draft decree with Frankfurter's own changes in pencil, along with related unique documents in the Frankfurter and Warren papers, has helped scholars analyze the evolution of the *Brown* case.

REMEMBERING THURGOOD MARSHALL

Long before President Lyndon Baines Johnson appointed him the first African-American Supreme Court justice in 1967, Thurgood Marshall (1908–1993) had established himself as the nation's leading legal civil rights advocate. After receiving his law degree from Howard University in 1933, he joined the legal staff of the NAACP about 1936 and between 1940 and 1961 served as head of the organization's Legal Defense and Educational Fund, which he created. In 1954 Marshall achieved national recognition for his work on *Brown v. Board of Education of Topeka*, the landmark Supreme Court decision that ruled public school segregation unconstitutional. In 1961 President John F. Kennedy appointed Marshall to the U.S. Court of Appeals, and four years later President Johnson named him solicitor general of the United States. In 1967 he joined the Supreme Court led by Chief Justice Earl Warren. For twenty-five years, until his retirement in 1991, Marshall led the legal fight to end racial discrimination in America. The Library holds a significant collection of his personal papers, both in the NAACP Legal Defense Fund Collection and in the Thurgood Marshall Papers.

Editorial cartoonist Paul Conrad (b. 1924) created this poignant tribute to Marshall upon Marshall's death in 1993. Creator of drawings notable for their potent political message, strong graphic style, spare compositions, and conceptual clarity, Conrad began his professional career in 1950 as an editorial cartoonist at the *Denver Post*. In 1964 he went to work for the *Los Angeles Times*, where he served as chief editorial cartoonist until 1993. Conrad won Pulitzer Prizes in 1964, 1971, and 1984.

THURGOOD MARSHALL 1908-1993

40.

AMERICAN ENTOMOLOGY

Each moss,
Each shell, each crawling insect, holds a rank
Important in the plan of Him who fram'd
This scale of being
      —Stillingfleet

This epigram graces the three-volume work *American Entomology: or Descriptions of the Insects of North America* (1824–28), the masterwork of Thomas Say (1787–1834), the father of American entomology. The engraving of the butterfly *Papilio turnus* reproduced here is typical of the meticulously detailed and beautifully conceived plates throughout the work. The drawings were done either by Say himself, or, as in this case, by Titian Ramsay Peale (1799–1885), the youngest son of Charles Willson Peale, based on observations taken from nature in the course of various expeditions to the South, the Rocky Mountains, the Minnesota River Basin, and Mexico. After finishing this work, Say went on to publish another definitive work, on American shells, and approached the subject with the same spirit of adventure and reverence that informed his work on insects. As he wrote, "It is an enterprise that may be compared to that of a pioneer or early settler in a strange land," and he did much to advance Americans' understanding of the natural world they encountered as they moved inexorably across the continent.

Son of a wealthy Quaker merchant, Say himself chose to sacrifice material comforts for the sake of science and was chronically ill from the malnutrition he experienced as a young man. In the 1830s he followed British philosopher Robert Owen to Indiana, where Owen established the utopian community of New Harmony. While the utopian experiment failed and Owen returned to England, Say remained in New Harmony and made it the base for all his scientific expeditions.

THE EARLIEST PHOTOGRAPHIC PORTRAIT

Robert Cornelius's 1839 self-portrait is the earliest extant American photographic portrait. Working outdoors to take advantage of the light, Cornelius (1809–1893) stood before his camera in the yard behind his family's lamp and chandelier store in Philadelphia, hair askew and arms folded across his chest, and looked off into the distance as if trying to imagine what his portrait would look like.

Early studio daguerreotypes required long exposure times, ranging from three to fifteen minutes, making the process highly impractical for portraiture. After Cornelius and his silent partner, Dr. Paul Beck Goddard, opened a daguerreotype studio in Philadelphia about May 1840, their improvements to the daguerreotype process enabled them to make portraits in a matter of seconds. Cornelius operated his studio for two and a half years before returning to work for his family's thriving gas light fixture business.

Invented in 1839, the daguerreotype was the first photographic process commercially available in the United States. Considered a democratic medium, photography provided the middle class with an opportunity to attain affordable portraits. Painting required considerable training, expensive materials, and long sittings, making a painted likeness a costly proposition that only the well-to-do could afford. While portrait painters and miniaturists, anxious about their livelihood, claimed that a photograph could not reveal the soul of the sitter, photographers extolled the accuracy of the photographic medium. This debate raged until the beginning of the twentieth century.

The Cornelius self-portrait is part of the Marian S. Carson Collection at the Library of Congress, one of the most important collections of early Americana in the nation. In addition to some of the earliest photographs taken in the United States, the collection contains several thousand manuscripts, including unpublished documents pertaining to the Continental Congresses, unique broadsides issued by the early Congresses and state governments, and many fine graphic images, including an important archive of drawings by nineteenth-century documentary artist James Queen.

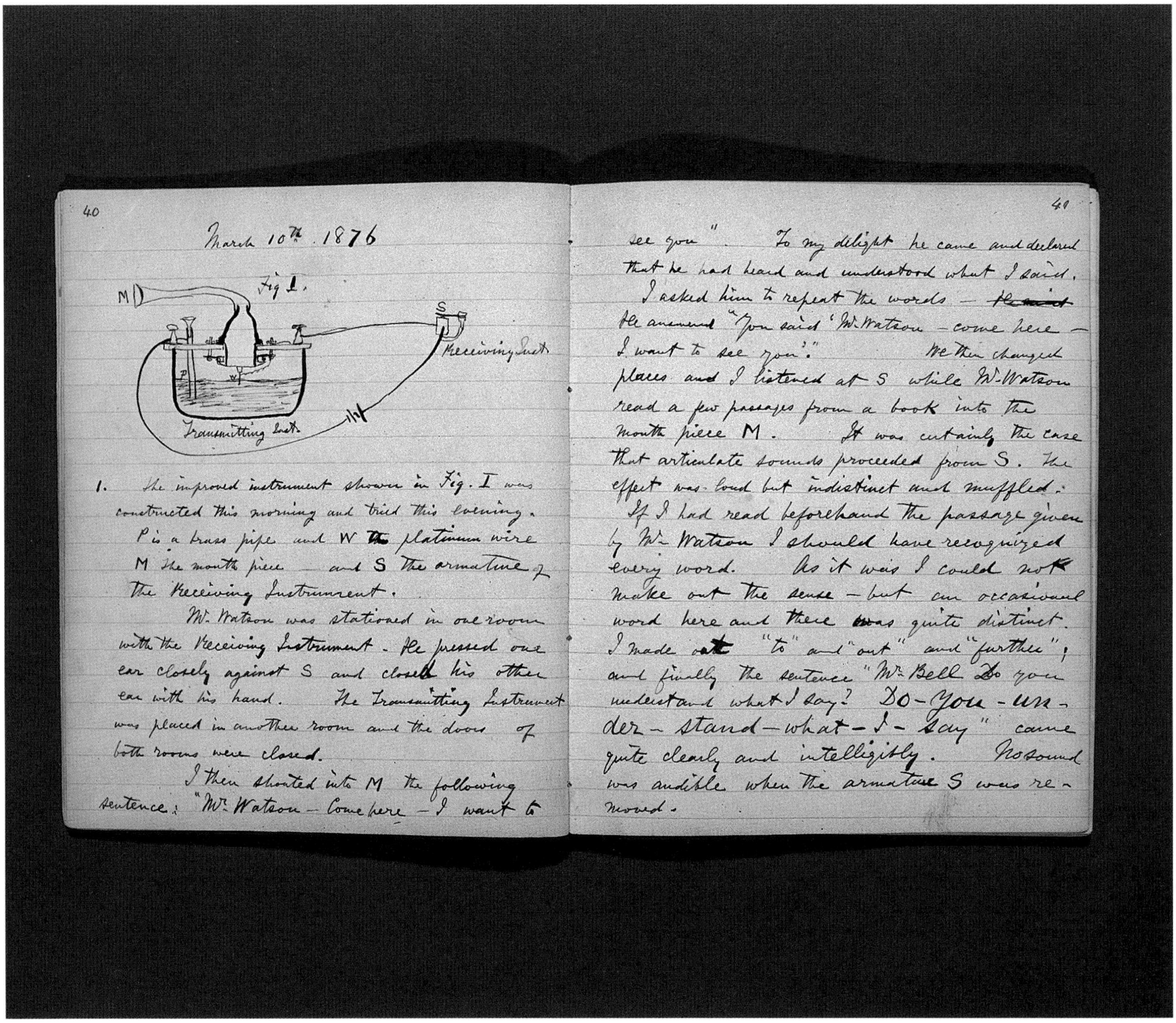

March 10th 1876

Fig I.

M — S Receiving Inst.

Transmitting Inst.

1. The improved instrument shown in Fig. I was constructed this morning and tried this evening.

P is a brass pipe and W the platinum wire M the mouth piece — and S the armature of the Receiving Instrument.

Mr. Watson was stationed in one room with the Receiving Instrument. He pressed one ear closely against S and closed his other ear with his hand. The Transmitting Instrument was placed in another room and the doors of both rooms were closed.

I then shouted into M the following sentence: "Mr. Watson — come here — I want to

see you". To my delight he came and declared that he had heard and understood what I said.

I asked him to repeat the words — He answered "You said 'Mr. Watson — come here — I want to see you'." We then changed places and I listened at S while Mr. Watson read a few passages from a book into the mouth piece M. It was certainly the case that articulate sounds proceeded from S. The effect was loud but indistinct and muffled.

If I had read beforehand the passage given by Mr. Watson I should have recognized every word. As it was I could not make out the sense — but an occasional word here and there was quite distinct. I made out "to" and "out" and "further"; and finally the sentence "Mr. Bell Do you understand what I say? Do — You — un — der — stand — what — I — say" came quite clearly and intelligibly. No sound was audible when the armature S was removed.

"MR. WATSON—COME HERE"

Alexander Graham Bell's notebook entry of March 10, 1876, describes the first successful experiment with the telephone in which he spoke through the instrument to his assistant, Thomas A. Watson, in the next room. Bell writes, "I then shouted into M [the mouthpiece] the following sentence: 'Mr. Watson—come here—I want to see you.' To my delight he came and declared that he had heard and understood what I said."

Bell was born into a family deeply interested in the problems of speech. Both his father and grandfather were teachers of elocution, and throughout his life, Bell had a keen interest in teaching the deaf to speak. Both his mother and the woman he married—Mabel Hubbard, one of his pupils—were deaf.

The Bell Papers were donated to the Library of Congress by his heirs on June 2, 1975, the centenary of the day Bell discovered the principle that made the invention of the telephone possible. This extraordinarily rich collection totals about 130,000 items and documents in great detail Bell's entire career, ranging from his work on the telephone to his interests in aeronautics and physics.

MUSIC MACHINES

In the late 1880s, German immigrant Emile Berliner (1851–1929), working in Washington, D.C., created a new medium for sound recording and playback, the flat disc "Gramophone." While Thomas Edison's 1877 phonograph was "a wonderful invention," in the words of a contemporary *Scientific American*, in its original tinfoil form it was impractical for common use. Edison soon devoted his energy to development of the incandescent light. But about the same time that Berliner was creating the gramophone, Alexander Graham Bell's Volta Laboratory and Edison's laboratory resumed work on development of the phonograph. (The word, "phonograph," was Edison's trade name for his device, which played cylinders rather than discs. The cylinder invention patented by Bell's Volta Laboratory was called the "graphophone.")

According to its donor, Mrs. Isabelle S. Sayers, this Gramophone machine of the mid-1890s was owned by Thomas Edison himself. While Edison probably saw little threat to his phonograph in this crude machine, discs would far outsell cylinders by 1910. Berliner's January 1895 List of Plates, shown next to the Gramophone, describes the typical range of music and speech that could be heard on cylinders as well as on discs at that time. The disc on the Gramophone machine seen here is the first recording of John Philip Sousa's "Stars and Stripes Forever," recorded for Berliner only thirteen days after the premiere of the march. Generous descendants of Berliner have entrusted the Library with preservation of more than five hundred published and unpublished Berliner discs along with the inventor's laboratory notebooks, business and legal papers, and personal scrapbooks.

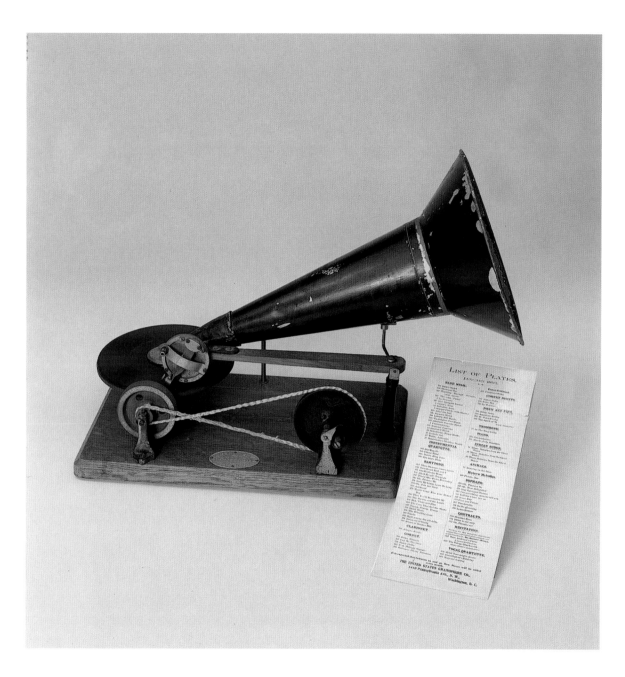

Edison Kinetoscopic Record of a Sneeze
Taken & Copyrighted by W.K.L.Dickson
Orange N.J. — Jan. 7th 94

FRED OTT'S SNEEZE

Thomas A. Edison began thinking about the development of motion pictures in 1888 after studying the successful motion-sequence still photographic experiments of Eadweard Muybridge and Étienne-Jules Marey. By early 1889, Edison had conceived the ambitious notion that it must be possible to record motion as perceived by the human eye and play it back in real time. His idea was to go beyond his predecessors, who had adapted the existing photographic equipment of the day to record brief sequences of motion, and invent an entirely new technology to do "for the eye what the phonograph does for the ear."

To turn his new invention into reality, Edison assigned responsibility for day-to-day development to one of his best assistants, a young Englishman named W. K. L. Dickson. By June of 1891, Dickson produced a series of successful experimental motion pictures that were shown to visiting groups at the Edison laboratory in New Jersey. Over the next two years Dickson worked to perfect the two basic machines required for successful motion pictures: a device to record moving images, which he and Edison called the Kinetograph; and a machine to view the results, which they called the Kinetoscope. A major problem that slowed Dickson's work in the beginning was the nonexistence in the commercial marketplace of another essential invention—motion picture film stock. After Eastman Kodak began supplying quantities of reliable film stock in the fall of 1893, the road to commercial development of the movies was opened.

The Edison Kinetoscopic Record of a Sneeze is one of a series of short films made by Dickson in January 1894 for advertising purposes. The star is Fred Ott, an Edison employee known to his fellow workers in the laboratory for his comic sneezing and other gags. This item was received in the Library of Congress on January 9, 1894, as a copyright deposit from W. K. L. Dickson and is the earliest surviving copyrighted motion picture.

FIRST FLIGHT

The Wright Brothers systematically photographed the prototypes and tests of their various flying machines. Their historic first powered flight near Kitty Hawk, North Carolina, in December 1903 was no exception. The camera, operated by an attendant from a nearby lifesaving station, captured their plane at the instant of takeoff with Orville at the controls. The craft soared to an altitude of 2 feet, traveled 120 feet, and landed twelve seconds later.

The papers of Wilbur (1867–1912) and Orville (1871–1948) Wright were given to the Library in 1949 by the executors of Orville Wright's estate. Over the years the Library has received additional materials through gifts and transfers, and altogether the collection comprises diaries and notebooks, family papers, general correspondence, subject files, scrapbooks, and more than 1,100 photographic images, including 300 original glass plate negatives.

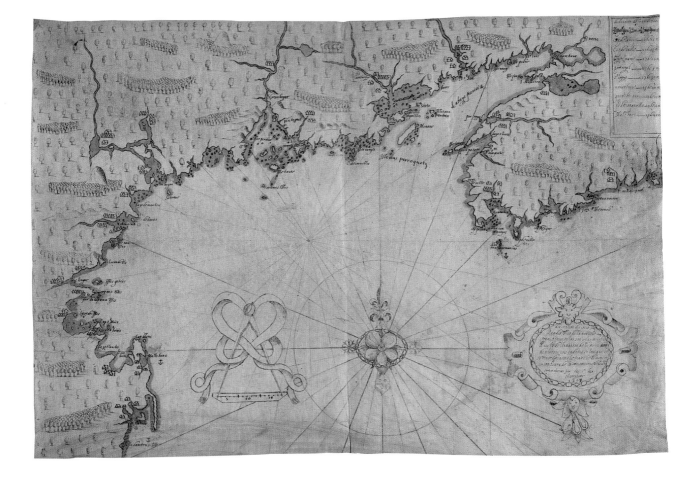

98

CHAMPLAIN PUTS NEW ENGLAND ON THE MAP

This unique exploration document, originally intended for presentation to the king of France, was compiled by Samuel de Champlain (1567–1635), founder of New France. One of the great cartographic treasures of America, it provides the first thorough delineation of the New England and Canadian coast from Cape Sable to Cape Cod. It shows Port Royal; Frenchman Bay; the St. John, St. Croix, Penobscot, and Kennebec Rivers; and many offshore islands—including Mount Desert, which Champlain himself named. The place names and coastline correspond closely to Champlain's narrative in his *Voyages*, published in 1613.

Champlain personally designed and drew this portolan-style chart on vellum. Most charts of the time were drawn by professional cartographers who depended on information obtained from explorers, navigators, and cosmographers. In contrast, Champlain based this chart entirely on his own exploration and observations, including interviews with Native Americans, and on his own mathematical calculations.

A number of habitations are shown along the shoreline, the larger ones representing French settlements and the smaller ones Native American villages. At Port Royal a turreted fort is shown, signifying a European settlement. Forests are represented by stylized drawings of trees, singly and in groups. Hill symbols indicate higher elevations visible from the shore. Dangerous shoals are shown as groups of small dots, and anchors represent locations where Champlain himself dropped anchor.

In 1883 the Bibliothèque Nationale in Paris purchased from a monk in Nantes a precious atlas containing Champlain's chart. Later the chart came into the possession of Henry Harrisse, a distinguished lawyer, historian, and bibliographer, who built a remarkable collection of maps, publications, and papers pertaining to the early exploration of America. Harrisse bequeathed his entire collection to the Library of Congress in 1915.

WASHINGTON'S 1749 PLAN OF ALEXANDRIA

George Washington (1732–1799), best known as a planter, soldier, and statesman, was trained as a surveyor during his late teenage years and practiced surveying in the western part of Virginia during the 1750s. Recent inventories indicate that he drew or annotated at least 150 maps during his lifetime. Of these, more than forty are found in various collections of the Library of Congress. Most of these pertain to land surveys in western Virginia, military operations in southwestern Pennsylvania, and surveys of his lands near Mount Vernon, Virginia.

When Washington was about seventeen years old, he prepared this manuscript plan of Alexandria, Virginia, as well as a similar map of the town site before the streets and lots were laid out. The town, which was formally established July 13, 1749, consisted of eighty-four lots, most of which were one-half acre in size. The site for this new town focused on a tobacco inspection warehouse and the stores of several Scottish merchants, located on the Potomac River just north of Great Hunting Creek in a small community that was originally known as Belhaven.

It is possible that Washington prepared this map while he was apprenticed to the county surveyor John West, whom he assisted in surveying the town boundaries and lots. He apparently prepared the map to send to his half-brother Lawrence, who was in England at the time, to show him the two town lots that had been purchased for him.

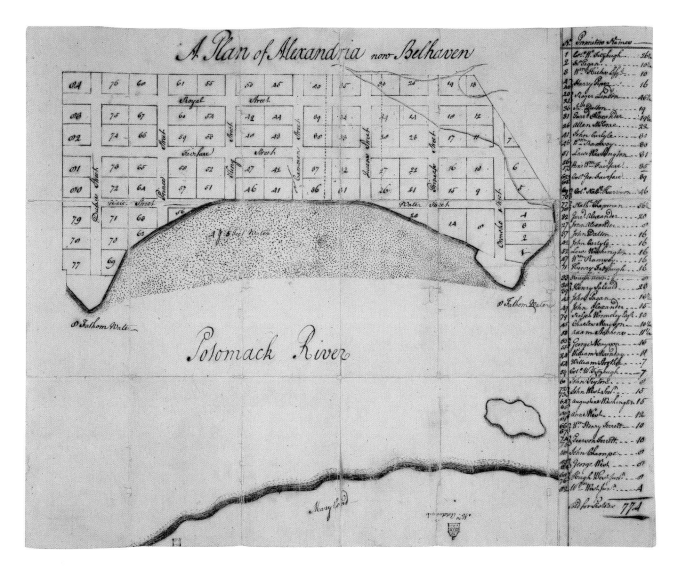

A Plan of Alexandria now Belhaven

Potomack River

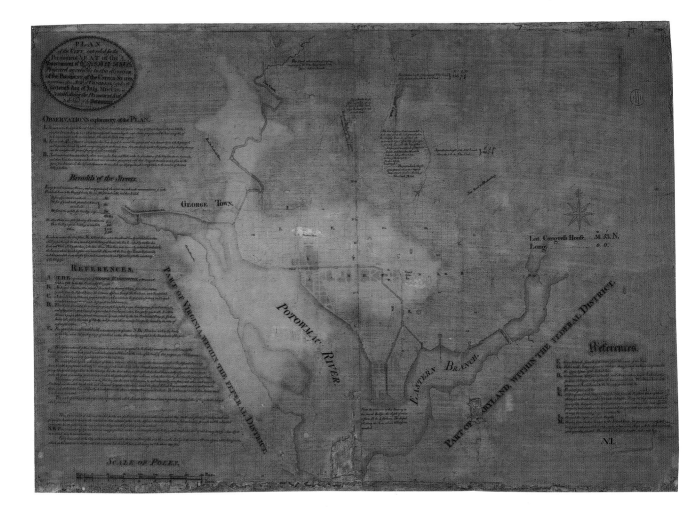

L'ENFANT'S CAPITAL PLAN

Pierre-Charles L'Enfant's 1791 plan for the city of Washington is one of the great landmarks in city planning. It was, L'Enfant claimed, "a plan whol[l]y new," designed from its inception to serve as the framework for the capital city of the new nation beginning in the year 1800. Its scheme of broad radiating avenues connecting significant focal points, its open spaces, and its grid pattern of streets oriented north, south, east, and west is still the plan against which all modern land use proposals for the nation's capital are considered.

L'Enfant (1754–1825) was born in France and educated as an architect and engineer. Caught up in the spirit of the American Revolutionary War, he came to America at the age of twenty-two and served with honor as an officer in the Corps of Engineers of the Continental army. On September 11, 1789, he wrote to President George Washington in order "to sollicit [sic] the favor of being Employed in the Business" of designing the new city. At this early date, L'Enfant already perceived "that the plan should be drawn on such a scale as to leave room for that aggrandizement & embellishment which the increase of the wealth of the Nation will permit it to pursue at any period how ever remote."

"An Act for establishing the temporary and permanent seat of the Government of the United States" was signed into law on July 16, 1790. After giving cursory consideration to other locations, George Washington selected a site for the seat of government with which he was very familiar—the banks of the Potomac River at the confluence of its Eastern Branch, just above his home at Mount Vernon. Selected by Washington to prepare a ground plan for the new city, L'Enfant arrived in Georgetown on March 9, 1791, and submitted his report and plan to the president about August 26, 1791. It is believed that this plan is the one that is preserved in the Library of Congress.

After showing L'Enfant's manuscript to Congress, the president retained custody of the original drawing until December 1796, when he transferred it to the City Commissioners of Washington, D.C. One hundred and twenty-two years later, on November 11, 1918, the map was presented to the Library of Congress for safekeeping.

In 1991, to commemorate the two hundredth anniversary of the plan, the Library of Congress, in cooperation with the National Geographic Society, the National Park Service, and the United States Geological Survey, published an exact-size, full-color facsimile and a computer-assisted reproduction of the original manuscript plan. These reproductions are the Library's first facsimiles to be based on photography and electronic enhancement technology. During this process, it was possible to record faint editorial annotations made by Thomas Jefferson, which are now virtually illegible on the original map.

LEWIS AND CLARK

The Library has a significant collection of manuscript and published maps documenting the expedition of Meriwether Lewis (1774–1809) and William Clark (1770–1838) to the Pacific Northwest from 1803 to 1806. These include published maps issued with the final reports of the expedition, interim composite maps showing the progress of the expedition, and maps used or consulted in planning the expedition.

One of the reasons the Lewis and Clark expedition succeeded in traversing the northwestern portion of North America and reaching the Pacific Ocean was because the leaders meticulously consulted the best carto-graphic sources that were available at the beginning of the nineteenth century to create a composite image of the geography of the western portion of North America. Shown here is a section of a composite map drawn in 1803 by Nicholas King, a War Department copyist, from published and manuscript sources, at the request of Thomas Jefferson and Secretary of the Treasury Albert Gallatin. The map reflects the geographical concepts of government leaders on the eve of the expedition. It is believed that Lewis and Clark carried this map on their journey at least as far as the Mandan-Hidatsa villages on the Missouri River, where Lewis annotated in brown ink additional infor-mation obtained from fur traders.

This map, as well as twelve other manuscript maps that are thought to have belonged to William Clark, was transferred to the Library of Congress in 1925 from the Office of Indian Affairs.

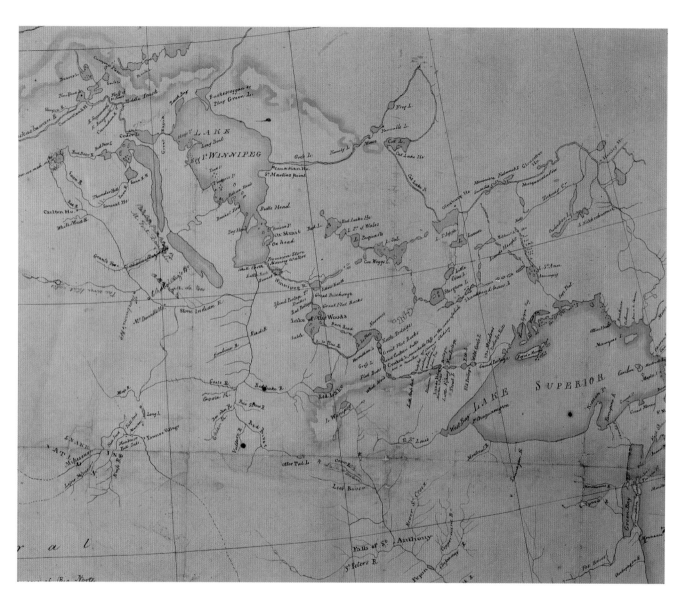

THE FIRST AMERICAN GLOBES

The three globes shown here were produced by James Wilson, America's first commercial globe maker. Born in New Hampshire in 1763, he spent much of his adult life as a farmer and blacksmith in nearby Vermont. After seeing a pair of terrestrial and celestial globes at Dartmouth College, he decided to make his own. He set about learning geography from an encyclopedia he purchased for the purpose and learned engraving from an experienced engraver of maps. Around 1810 he produced his first globe, and by 1818 he and his sons had established an "artificial globe manufactory" in Albany, New York, where they produced globes of three-inch, nine-inch, and thirteen-inch diameters.

In 1827 he brought his globes down to Washington, D.C., to display to Congress. On his business card he wrote that he was "now exhibiting for public inspection at the United States Library" a pair of thirteen-inch globes, and claimed he was "the original manufacturer of Globes in this country, and has brought the art to such a degree of perfection, as to supersede altogether the necessity of importation of that article from abroad."

The two smaller globes shown here are an undated pair of three-inch terrestrial and celestial globes probably created in the 1820s. They were purchased by the Library in 1940 from Harold F. Wilson, a descendant of the globe maker. The larger thirteen-inch globe is one of Wilson's earliest dated globes (1811), and was a gift to the Library in 1991 by the estate of the noted globe and map collector, Howard Welsh.

INDIAN SETTLEMENTS OF EASTERN WISCONSIN

This map of a part of eastern Wisconsin, probably made by a French voyageur, was carried by explorer, geologist, ethnologist, Indian agent, and Superintendent of Indian Affairs for Michigan Henry Rowe Schoolcraft (1793–1864), who annotated it in the course of an expedition he made in the summer of 1831. Sent by the governor of the Michigan Territory, Schoolcraft was to take a census of the Chippewa and Sioux settlements in the upper Mississippi River country and try to negotiate a settlement between the hostile tribes. Schoolcraft added the place names of Native American villages, their chiefs' names, and pertinent census data. The reverse orientation of the map, with the south at the top, probably reflects the descent of the voyageur into the region from the north.

An account of this expedition is included in Schoolcraft's *Narrative of an Expedition Through the Upper Mississippi to Itasca Lake, The Actual Source of the River; Embracing an Exploratory Trip through the St. Croix and Burntwood (or Broule) Rivers; in 1832*, printed in 1834. His original manuscript of the book is a part of his papers in the Manuscript Division.

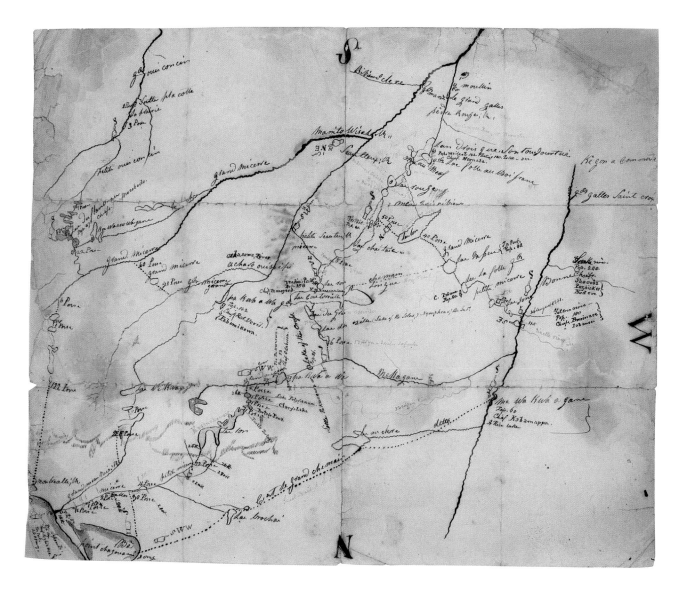

MAPPING THE CIVIL WAR

Of the more than 2,200 Civil War maps in the Library's holdings, probably the most outstanding materials are found in the collection of maps compiled and collected by Jedediah Hotchkiss (1828–1899), a topographic engineer in the Confederate States Army who prepared maps and provided geographic intelligence for Thomas J. "Stonewall" Jackson, Robert E. Lee, Richard Ewell, Jubal Early, and John B. Gordon. This collection is important not only because it documents the work of one of the most gifted cartographers of the Civil War, but also because it represents the full range of cartographic production, incorporating 341 field notebooks, detailed reconnaissance maps, and finely drawn after-battle maps, as well as maps annotated by Jackson, Lee, and others, indicating their use in planning campaigns. The Library's Manuscript Division holds a complementary twenty-seven-thousand-item manuscript collection, including diaries, correspondence, and notebooks compiled by Hotchkiss.

Born and educated in New York State, Hotchkiss moved to Virginia's Shenandoah Valley in 1847. At the outbreak of the Civil War, he offered his services to the Confederate army and was assigned to the staff of General Jackson as a topographic engineer of the Valley District, Department of Virginia. One of his most remarkable achievements was the preparation of a detailed topographic map of the Shenandoah Valley, measuring 7½ by 3 feet.

Three items representative of Hotchkiss's work are illustrated here. The closed field notebook shows his inscription on the cover: "This volume is my field sketch book that I used during the Civil War. Most of the sketches were made on horseback just as they now appear. The colored pencils used were kept in the places fixed on the outside of the other cover. These topographical sketches were often used in conferences with Generals Jackson, Ewell and Early." Another field notebook, recording the positions of the Second Corps of the Army of Northern Virginia during 1864–65 engagements, is open to a page of rough sketch notes. The finished manuscript map covers the area from the southern Shenandoah Valley to Washington, D.C., and was one of the maps prepared for an atlas to accompany the final report on the campaign of 1864. The atlas was not published, but a number of the maps were reproduced in the *Atlas to Accompany the Official Records of the Union and Confederate Armies, 1891–95.*

The collection was purchased by the Library in 1948, from Mrs. R. E. Christian of Deerfield, Virginia, the granddaughter and last surviving descendant of Hotchkiss.

SHOOTING THE COLORADO

In 1871 Lt. George Wheeler was put in charge of the United States Geological Surveys West of the One Hundredth Meridian, the fourth official exploration of the West. Wheeler was tasked with collecting an accurate physical description of parts of eastern Nevada and Arizona, including the topography and mineral resources, information on resident Native Americans, and other facts valuable for settlement and economic exploitation. One of the first assistants he hired was the highly experienced field photographer and surveyor Timothy O'Sullivan (1840–1882).

Probably born in Ireland, O'Sullivan joined Mathew Brady's Washington, D.C., studio as an apprentice photographer about 1856 or 1857. It was on the bloody battlefields of the Civil War, working first for Brady and then for Alexander Gardner, that O'Sullivan won his reputation for technical proficiency in the tedious wet collodion photographic process and for artistry in the field. After having witnessed the cataclysm of his country torn by civil war, O'Sullivan satisfied a lust for adventure by joining government-sponsored missions intended to support America's rush to fulfill its Manifest Destiny. O'Sullivan worked on assignments with geologist Clarence King's survey of the Fortieth Parallel and the Navy's Darien Survey in Panama before being chosen for Wheeler's team.

Hoping to test the limits of practical navigation by measuring the width and velocity of the Colorado River, Wheeler commanded a party of three boats for the month-long journey. The trip up the Colorado to Diamond Creek in the Grand Canyon was two hundred miles against a strong current. Two boats in Wheeler's party—including O'Sullivan's boat, "The Picture"—accomplished the feat of reaching the highest point believed to have been navigated at that time, with Wheeler's own boat lost in the effort. "The Picture" is shown in this photograph with a tiny figure aboard, who mediates between the viewer and the dramatically lit landscape of stilled water and harsh rock walls. The photograph provides proof that the crew survived the long and tortuous journey through the mysterious canyon, while at the same time implying how they must have been humbled by the chilling experience.

T. H. O'Sullivan, Phot.   N° 8

BLACK CAÑON, COLORADO RIVER, FROM CAMP 8, LOOKING ABOVE.

ARIZONA, AS FROM ABOVE

This physical relief map of the state of Arizona is representative of the strikingly beautiful cartographic paintings created during the 1950s and 1960s by Hal Shelton, one of America's foremost twentieth-century innovators in cartographic design and relief representation, for use as base maps for aerial navigation charts. Since the paintings were created for duplication purposes, they still retain tape, labels, and registration markers, which guided the printers in applying other layers of information needed on the aeronautical charts.

Shelton's goal was to create three-dimensional relief paintings that would reproduce the natural colors of the physical landscape, as seen by pilots flying overland, as accurately as possible. He applied acrylic paints using an oscillating needle-air brush on zinc plates, which were first etched with cartographic base information, including contour lines. He shaped landforms through tonal shading—that is, by grading individual colors from light to dark, creating the appearance of shadows. These maps were not only widely adopted by pilots, but were also used as teaching aids in schools and colleges, as well as by the National Aeronautics and Space Administration to index photographs taken on early space missions.

This image of Arizona shows the deeply dissected plateau region encompassing the Grand Canyon of the Colorado River in the northwestern part of the state, as well as the Painted Desert, represented as an orange-colored arc in the north central part of the state. The south central part bears a rectangular grid pattern of greens and browns representing the irrigated agricultural lands along the Gila River in the vicinity of Phoenix.

This map, as well as twenty-eight other original paintings by Hal Shelton, were part of a gift to the Library in 1984 from The H. M. Gousha Company.

☆ Imagination ☆

Arts, the realm of the imagination, were cultivated at Monticello by a man who was a musician, a prose stylist, a theorist of poetical metrics, and a collector of paintings and statues. Architecture was his favorite art, since it was an ordering framework within which all the other arts could find their place—in the music room, libraries, galleries, and furnishings that proceed from and then feed the human imagination.

As many critics have noticed, the work of Frank Lloyd Wright would have been especially interesting to Jefferson. Both men were interested in native materials, technological advances, the blending of geometric purity and practical daily use.

The violin and harpsichord concerts at Monticello were distant in style, but not in their basic concept, from the jazz of Duke Ellington and Frank Sinatra, the marches of Sousa, the Broadway hits of Gershwin and Berlin and Bernstein.

Sports are one art Jefferson showed no interest in. He was not, like Washington, an athlete—though he admired good horsemanship (and called Washington the best horseman he ever saw, a high compliment in Virginia). Is sport—mere bodily performance—an art? No one can doubt it who saw the control over the body achieved by Martha Graham or George Balanchine, in the ballets whose scores we see here (*Appalachian Spring* and *Agon*). Athletes, like ballet artists, shape achievement with their bodies. Such a developed skill, based on discipline and timing, is too practical to be called a science, too creative *not* to be called an art. When the matter is put in those terms, even Jefferson would have recognized that the great ball player is as deft at ball and bat as the great musician is with fiddle and bow.

G. WILLS

A DESIGN FOR THE U.S. CAPITOL

George Washington and Thomas Jefferson sought the best talent available for the design of the U.S. Capitol, the architectural centerpiece of the new federal district. In March of 1793, at the end of a design competition, the French-trained architect Stephen Hallet (1755–1825) submitted this masterful rendering. Here we see inside the great "Conference Room," where the young nation's two legislative bodies, the House and the Senate, were to meet in joint session to work out their differences. It is also the space where the president presumably would have delivered his addresses on the "State of the Union."

Although the judges were enthusiastic about Hallet's design, a design submitted by William Thornton (1759–1828) was awarded first prize. A meeting held in Philadelphia on July 15, 1793, led to a compromise in which Thornton's design for the exterior was combined with Hallet's designs for the interiors. The "Conference Room" remained a part of the plans until it was removed by Thomas Jefferson and architect Benjamin Henry Latrobe after 1806, possibly because legislators decided that the arduous work of conference and compromise would be better done in the more informal spaces in the building, or possibly for the practical reason that the young government could not afford to build such a grandly conceived room. Nevertheless, Hallet's domed form is echoed today in the Capitol's rotunda.

AN AMERICAN SYMBOL

Between 1810 and 1840, painter and printmaker John Rubens Smith (1775–1849) traveled the eastern seaboard of the United States, creating a life portrait of the young republic. Smith sketched cities and towns, rivers, roads, bridges, and mills. His drawings captured the spirit and energy of the new nation during a period of enormous growth and optimism. The nearly completed U.S. Capitol must have seemed to Smith a particularly poignant symbol of American idealism and ambition. He rendered it from virtually every angle, including this finished view from about 1830. The cows grazing on what is now the Mall offer surprising visual evidence that America's rural character persisted even as urbanization and the Industrial Revolution transformed the nation.

INSIDE THE TOWN CHURCH

One of the founders and the first president of the American Institute of Architects, Richard Upjohn (1802–1878) was a key figure in introducing the Gothic Revival to the United States and in defining the form and appearance of American ecclesiastical architecture. The great flowering of the Episcopal Church in the United States in the 1840s and 1850s resulted in numerous and widespread commissions to Upjohn for church buildings. These built works and those illustrated in his *Rural Architecture* (1852) and other publications served as patterns for countless buildings throughout the country. The nation's bountiful forests and newly mechanized and portable sawmills made his designs for wooden churches eminently practical for congregations in smaller towns and rural areas. Upjohn was especially daring and inventive in his use of simple board-and-batten cladding, producing designs that we see today as surprisingly modern in concept. His drawing for this church reveals the combination of his skills as an architect and his thorough understanding of the possibilities of wooden construction, learned from working as a carpenter early in his career.

THE VISIONARY GENIUS OF FRANK LLOYD WRIGHT

One of the greatest innovators in the history of architecture, Frank Lloyd Wright (1867–1959) experimented extensively with new design vocabularies and building systems in a wide range of materials during a career that spanned over seven decades, most of this continent, and several foreign countries. During the 1920s he designed a number of houses in California using precast "textile" concrete blocks reinforced by an internal system of metal bars. One such house was built in Hollywood for Dr. John Storer and now, over seventy years later, is regularly used in films and television programs to represent a future at which we have yet to arrive. Typically Wrightian is the joining of the structure to its site by a series of terraces that reach out into and reorder the landscape, making it an integral part of the architect's vision. This rendering dated 1923 is one of an important group of drawings donated to the Library by one of Wright's assistants, Donald D. Walker.

STARS AND STRIPES FOREVER

Hurrah for the flag of the free!
May it wave as our standard forever,
The gem of the land and the sea,
The banner of the right.
Let despots remember the day
When our fathers with mighty endeavor
Proclaimed as they marched to the fray
That by their might and by their right
It waves forever.
　　　　　—John Philip Sousa

"March music is for the feet, not for the head," John Philip Sousa once stated. "The Stars and Stripes Forever," composed in 1896, is indeed music for the feet, but it has also become a musical calling card for our nation. Sousa's genius lay in his skill as a composer of great melodies and his ability to fashion them into a cohesive and "organic" whole. "The Stars and Stripes Forever" gets people up on their feet, marching forward together.

On the composition of marches Sousa was unusually silent, but toward the end of his life he stated his philosophy of setting pen to paper in march time: "A march speaks to a fundamental rhythm in the human organization and is answered. A march stimulates every centre of vitality, wakens the imagination. . . . But a march must be good. It must be as free from padding as a marble statue. Every line must be carved with unerring skill. Once padded it ceases to be a march. There is no form of musical composition wherein the harmonic structure must be more clear-cut. The whole process is an exacting one. There must be a melody which appeals to the musical and the unmusical alike. There must be no confusion in counterpoint."

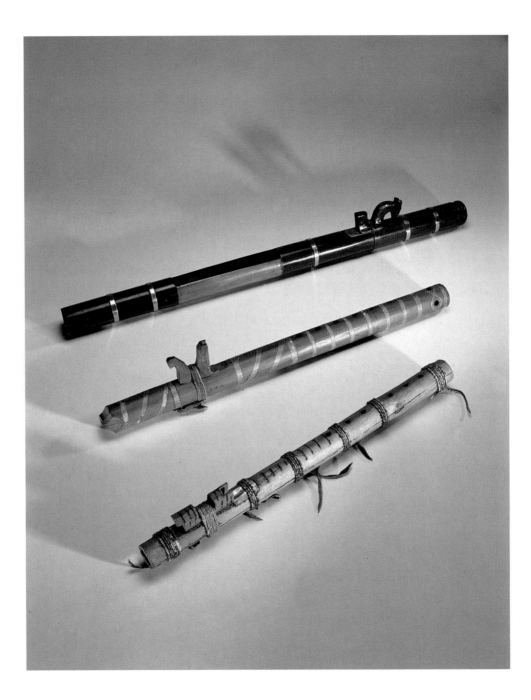

NATIVE AMERICAN FLUTES

Though unison singing accompanied by one or more drums or rattles is the more familiar musical mode, flutes played special roles in Native American music—enhancing ritual and serving as outlets for individual expression. Flutes ranged from simple whistles made of hollowed-out small animal bone, to large and colorfully decorated instruments made of carved wood and other elements lashed together. The latter were most common, and as instruments devoted to courting, religious, and healing uses, no two flutes were alike. Their sizes and forms depended on available materials and the talents of each individual flutist-craftsman. Even the placement of finger holes on the courting flutes was a personal choice. The resulting scale became the player's personal musical expression, and, as the flutes were used as solo instruments, there was no need for more consistent scales.

The examples of courting flutes shown here—made by (top to bottom) a Quapaw from Oklahoma; a Ute; and a Nebraska Winnebago—are among the approximately 120 instruments of Native American origin from over thirty tribal groups that form part of the Library's Miller Flute Collection. Dayton C. Miller (1866–1941), a professor of astronomy and physics, spent much of his life collecting flutes and primary material concerning the instrument's history and development. He bequeathed his collection of more than sixteen hundred flutes to the Library of Congress, and these instruments, along with books and related materials, are now in the Library's Music Division.

JELLY ROLL MORTON AND THE "FROG-I-MORE RAG"

Ferdinand Joseph "Jelly Roll" Morton (1885–1941) is generally acknowledged as jazz's first composer. The talents of this remarkable New Orleans jazz pioneer—composer, arranger, pianist—were exceeded only by his ego. He termed himself the inventor of jazz, claiming this honor in his extraordinary nine hours of recorded interviews with Alan Lomax for the Library of Congress Music Division's Archive of American Folk Song in 1938. In those interviews, constituting perhaps the first extended "oral history" ever created, Morton shows himself to be a brilliant raconteur: over his own piano vamps, he recalls turn-of-the-century life in New Orleans and illustrates the evolution of ragtime to jazz.

Morton probably wrote the "Frog-i-More Rag" in 1908 to accompany a fellow vaudevillian known as "Frog-i-More," a contortionist who performed in a frog costume. But Morton did not deposit the music for copyright until 1918, for fear that any form of public record was an invitation to purloin his ideas. The "Frog-i-More Rag" seen here, in Jelly Roll's own hand, is the first of many copyright deposits the Library holds for Morton. Morton recorded the rag twice in the spring of 1924, but only one of the recordings survives; it was not released until the 1940s. This particular issue was published in 1949 by a group of record collectors who revived the Paramount records imprint. Paramount was a historically and musically significant record label of the 1920s and early 1930s. The disc and the tinted photograph of Morton are from the Nesuhi Ertegun Collection of Jelly Roll Morton Recordings at the Library of Congress. The Ertegun Collection contains every commercial recording Morton ever made, all in their original 78-rpm disc format.

GERSHWIN'S CLASSIC AMERICAN OPERA

Porgy and Bess, an opera written by George Gershwin (1898–1937) in collaboration with DuBose Heyward (1885–1940) and Heyward's wife, Dorothy (1890–1961), is the one American opera to become fully established in the international opera repertory as well as in the popular musical imagination. Its tunes have become standards for jazz improvisation, and the lullaby "Summertime" has by now achieved the status of a folk song. *Porgy and Bess* is based on DuBose Heyward's 1925 novel *Porgy* and on the 1927 Broadway play of the same name by DuBose and Dorothy Heyward. Gershwin sketched the opera in 1934 and prepared the orchestra score (its opening page shown here) from September 1934 to September 1935.

The manuscript score-sketch of *Porgy and Bess* and the full orchestral-vocal score were given to the Library by Rose Gershwin, George and Ira Gershwin's mother, to whom George gave the manuscripts of all his major concert works after having them elegantly bound. The Library's Gershwin® Collection also includes considerable manuscript music for the Gershwin® stage musicals and material from their late songs for Hollywood musicals, with artfully crafted piano accompaniments in George's own hand.

SINATRA AUDITIONS

In 1935, the first year of radio network broadcasts of *Major Bowes' Amateur Hour*, more than thirty thousand acts auditioned for the talent contest program. One of the successful acts was the "Hoboken Four." The vocal quartet auditioned as "Frank Sinatra and the 3 Flashes," but was renamed, purportedly by Major Bowes himself. The act won the competition of the September 8, 1935, broadcast and joined one of Major Bowes's traveling vaudeville units. Sinatra soon left the tour to strike out on his own.

The Library holds a copy of nearly every radio and television network broadcast of the *Amateur Hour* program, which ran until 1970, and every successful application form for contestants on the radio series. Other *Amateur Hour* performers represented in the collection who went on to achieve stardom include Robert Merrill, Regina Resnick, Beverly Sills, Gladys Knight, Pat Boone, Jack Carter, Dorothy Collins, and Ann-Margret. Many believe that Maria Callas appeared on the radio program, but research has not substantiated this rumor.

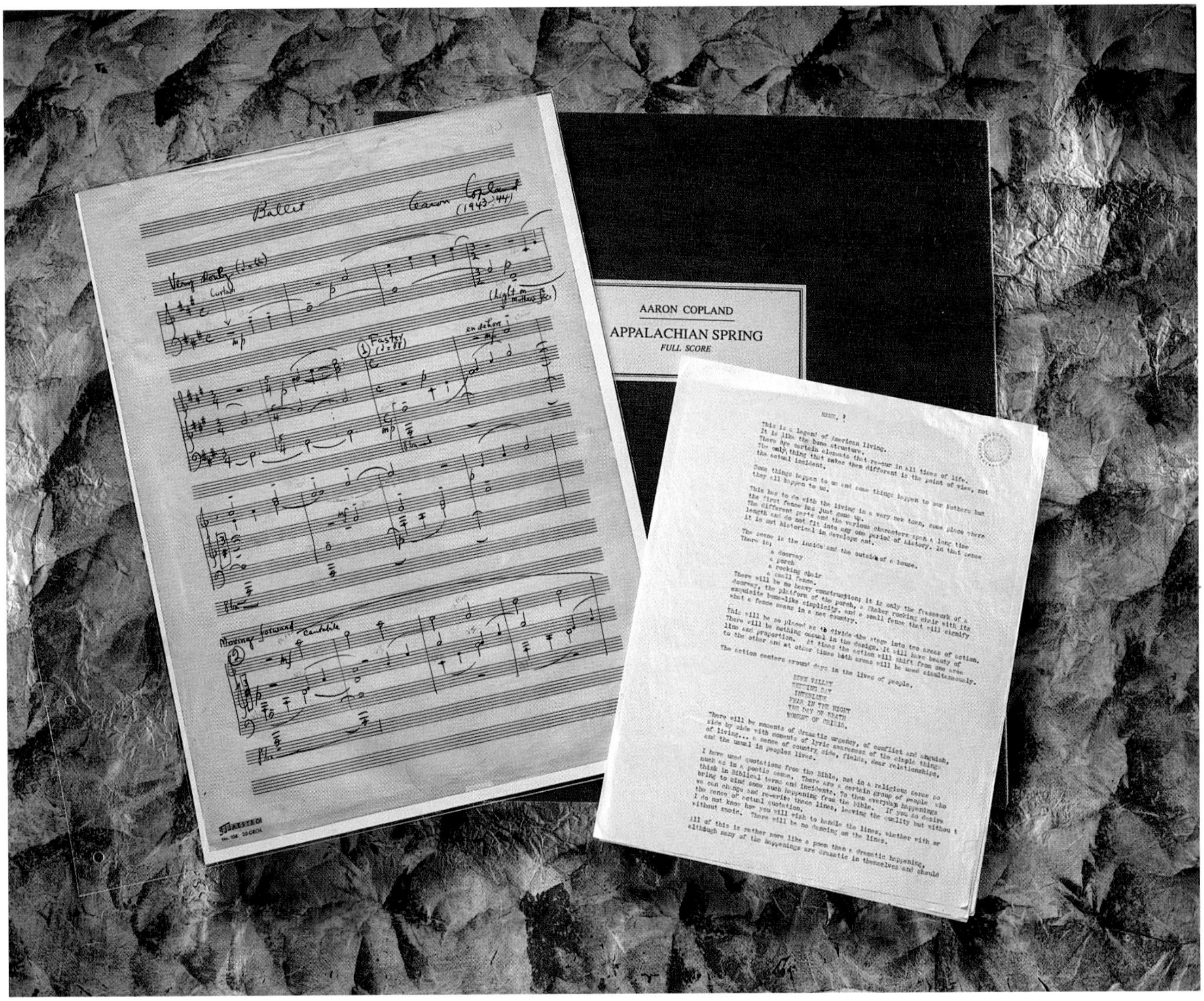
AARON COPLAND
APPALACHIAN SPRING
FULL SCORE

A BALLET FOR MARTHA

Appalachian Spring, a ballet with music by Aaron Copland and choreography by Martha Graham, was commissioned in 1942 by the Elizabeth Sprague Coolidge Foundation of the Library of Congress and first performed on October 30, 1944, at the Library's Coolidge Auditorium.

Awarded the 1944 Pulitzer Prize in music, this ballet, which "has to do with roots in so far as people can express them without telling an actual story" (Martha Graham's description), is regarded as one of the defining works for the American experience. The design of the dance emerged slowly, as is documented by Graham's three scripts for the work (none of them titled *Appalachian Spring*) in the Aaron Copland Collection of the Library of Congress.

The first script, sent to Copland in July 1942 and titled *Daughter of Colchis*, is basically a retelling of the Medea legend in terms of New England "about the time of a tale by Poe or Hawthorne." Copland found this libretto gloomy and suggested that they try something "less severe." Graham's second libretto—titled *House of Victory*—was sent to Copland in May 1943. This script begins to show the outlines of *Appalachian Spring* as we know it, but it is heavily involved with the Civil War, even to the presentation of a version of *Uncle Tom's Cabin* as a show-within-the-show. Copland thought the script viable but asked for revisions. The final script, this time untitled, was sent to him in July 1943.

Copland wrote *Appalachian Spring*—or rather his untitled "Ballet for Martha"—to Graham's final script. But when she heard the music Graham decided to redo the action yet again:

I have been working on your music. It is so beautiful and so wonderfully made. I have become obsessed by it. But I have also been doing a little cursing, too, as you probably did earlier over that not-so-good script. But what you did from that has made me change in many places. Naturally that will not do anything to the music, it is simply that the music made me change. It is so knit and of a completeness that it takes you into very strong hands and leads you into its own world. And there I am.

So, finally, there is no "script" for *Appalachian Spring*. There is only the dance.

A PHOTOGRAPH OF MUSIC ROYALTY

During the late 1930s *The Washington Post* was hesitant to pay staff photographers for the late-night hours required to accompany the paper's novice music columnist William Gottlieb on his postshow interviews with jazz musicians at various Washington, D.C., nightclubs. So Gottlieb, inspired by the new photojournalism of *Life* magazine, learned to take his own photographs. He covered the jazz and blues scene first for *The Washington Post* and later for *Down Beat*. He captured this image of Duke Ellington's charismatic presence after a performance at New York's Paramount Theater in the late 1940s. Ellington—his reflection caught in a dressing room mirror—looks fully the part of an American musical giant: debonair and handsome. Creator of such distinctive yet iconic classics as "Mood Indigo," "Sophisticated Lady," and "Satin Doll," Ellington considered his music as both personal expression and a continuation and reaffirmation of the African-American musical heritage.

The Gottlieb Photographic Collection contains approximately fifteen hundred images of eminent jazz musicians including Louis Armstrong, Ella Fitzgerald, and Thelonious Monk, and was purchased with funds from a bequest of Ira and Leonore Gershwin for use by the Music Division.

STRAVINSKY AND BALANCHINE

Igor Stravinsky's ballet *Agon* (meaning "contest") was first danced on December 1, 1957, by the New York City Ballet, with choreography by another Russian émigré artist, George Balanchine (1904–1983). The music had received its premiere in Los Angeles in a concert held the previous June, with Robert Craft conducting. As seen here on the title page of the holograph score, the composer dedicated the ballet to Balanchine and Lincoln Kirstein, cofounders of the New York City Ballet.

Agon is the third of three ballet collaborations between Stravinsky (1882–1971) and Balanchine, the other two being *Apollon Musagète* (1928) and *Orpheus* (1948). Unlike those previous works, *Agon* is plotless, an abstract ballet for eight female and four male dancers. Some of the dances were suggested by a description of seventeenth-century French court dances, to which the titles of movements, such as "Bransle Simple," "Bransle Gay," and "Bransle de Poitou," bear witness. Another influence was the music of the Second Vienna School, particularly Anton Webern. Stravinsky had written works using serial procedures within a tonal context, notably the *Cantata* of 1952, before beginning work on *Agon* in 1953. By the time he finished the ballet in April 1957, he had completed his *Canticum Sacrum*, which contains sections employing strict serial technique. *Agon* itself progresses from a basically diatonic, fanfarelike opening through a series of increasingly chromatic movements to a "Pas de deux" that speaks the language of the late, serial Stravinsky. Balanchine rose to the musical language of the "Pas de deux" with a dance for Diana Adams and Arthur Mitchell that became one of the defining moments of midcentury ballet. The ballet is the artistic and spiritual triumph of two artists who fled their homeland following the turbulence of revolution to seek artistic freedom of expression and who went on to transplant the musical and dance heritage of Imperial Russia onto American soil with spectacular results that forever changed dance.

"SOMETHING'S COMING"

My Fair Lady, a big Broadway hit in 1956, turned out to be the culmination of the Rodgers and Hammerstein tradition and the end of an era. *West Side Story*, staged in 1957, was the beginning of the next. Never before had dance been such an integral part of the storytelling of a musical; its tritone-laden score included propulsive Latin rhythms, angular, jazzy themes, five-part counterpoint, and a tone row. Based on Shakespeare's *Romeo and Juliet*, it was the first musical tragedy—what other musical ends each act with a dead body on the stage?

In addition to Leonard Bernstein's score, Jerome Robbins's choreography and direction, and Arthur Laurents's libretto, the show introduced Stephen Sondheim's work as a lyricist to Broadway audiences. According to Bernstein:

> *"Something's Coming" was born right out of a big long speech that Arthur wrote for Tony. It said how every morning he would wake up and reach for something, around the corner or down the beach. It was very late and we were in rehearsal when Steve and I realized that we needed a strong song for Tony earlier since he had none until "Maria," which was a love song. We had to have more delineation of him as a character. We were looking through this particular speech, and "Something's Coming" just seemed to leap off the page. In the course of the day we had written that song.*

The sketches and piano-vocal scores from *West Side Story* were among the gifts given to the Library by Bernstein during the 1960s. In 1992 his children generously donated the rest of the materials, including his annotated conducting score from the musical, that form his artistic legacy.

AN EXTRAORDINARY POETICAL GENIUS

The gifted young black poet Phillis Wheatley (1753?–1784) was celebrated as "the extraordinary poetical genius" of colonial New England even before this compilation of her poems was published in September 1773. Not yet eight years old when she was brought to America from Africa in 1761, Wheatley was educated by her mistress, and her first poem was published in a Rhode Island newspaper when she was only fourteen. Her pious elegies for prominent English and colonial leaders became popular and were often reprinted in colonial newspapers or as broadsides.

Wheatley's 1773 visit to London, ostensibly to improve her frail condition, was cut short by her mistress' failing health. Although she was entertained by William Legge, earl of Dartmouth, the abolitionist Grenville Sharpe, John Thornton, and Benjamin Franklin, Wheatley did not meet her patron, Selina Hastings, Countess of Huntingdon, to whom she dedicated her *Poems on Various Subjects, Religious and Moral*. The countess suggested including the frontispiece portrait of Wheatley in the book. It was probably drawn by the black painter Scipio Moorhead (servant to Rev. John Moorhead of Boston), whose creative talents are praised in one of Wheatley's poems. Wheatley was given her freedom shortly after returning from England, but attended her mistress until the woman's death in March 1774.

The Library holds copies of many editions of Wheatley's poems. Book collector George Livermore gave this copy of the first London edition to the distinguished American historian and collector Peter Force in 1850, and it subsequently came to the Library when the Library purchased the Peter Force Collection in 1867.

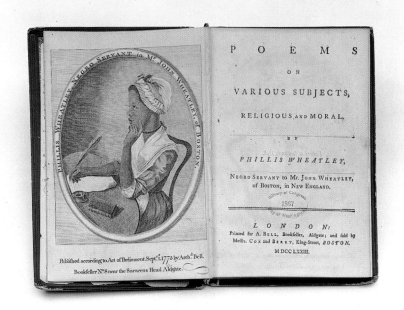

A CURIOUS HIEROGLYPHICK BIBLE

A touchstone of eighteenth-century American book illustration, this "curious" children's Bible contains nearly five hundred woodcuts made by American artists. The most ambitious woodcut book produced in America to that time, it is one of the sixty-five children's book titles made by the pioneer publisher of children's literature and pre-eminent early American printer Isaiah Thomas (1749–1831), who had learned the art of engraving while apprenticed in his youth to the Boston printer Zechariah Fowle. Only four copies of this remarkable piece of early Americana exist today.

A hieroglyphic Bible replaces some of the words of the text with pictures in an attempt to tell a story in a direct, simple, and interesting way. Such Bibles became very popular in the late eighteenth century as an easy means of teaching the Scripture to the young. In his preface to this volume, Thomas offers this first American hieroglyphic Bible, more extensively illustrated than its English prototype, as not only a pleasing method of teaching Bible lessons to children, but as "an easy Way of leading them on in Reading."

Printed in Worcester, Massachusetts, the book was inscribed by its first owner: "Enoch Brooks' Book, Princeton, March 13th, 1789." It is now in the Library's American Imprint Collection. English precursors and nineteenth-century American editions are found in the Bible Collection, a representative sampling of nearly fifteen hundred early editions and rare issues of Bibles in numerous languages.

In the Beginning ☉ created

the 🌊 and the 🌍

And the Earth was without Form and void, and Darkness was upon the Face of the Deep ; and the

of God moved upon the

In the Beginning *God* created the *Heaven* and the *Earth.* And the Earth was without Form and void, and Darkness was upon the Face of the Deep ; and the *Spirit* of God moved upon the *Waters.*

On the fourth Day

the Lord

commanded that the

should shine, the give her

and that the ✷✷✷ should be in Order. And gave them a Charge to do Service unto Man that was to be made.

On the fourth day the Lord commanded that the *Sun* should shine, the *Moon* give her *Light,* and that the *Stars* should be in Order. And gave them a Charge to do Service unto Man that was to be made.

O the bleeding drops of red!

O CAPTAIN! MY CAPTAIN!

BY WALT WHITMAN.

I.

O CAPTAIN! my captain! our fearful trip is done
The ship has weathered every rack, the prize we sought is won,
The port is near, the bells I hear, the people all exulting,
While follow eyes the steady keel, the vessel grim and daring.
    But O heart! heart! heart!
    ~~Leave you not the little spot~~
    Where on the deck my captain lies,
      Fallen cold and dead.

II.

O captain! my captain! rise up and hear the bells
Rise up! for you the flag is flung, for you the bugle trills:
For you bouquets and ribboned wreaths, for you the shores a-crowd-
      ing:
For you they call, the swaying mass, their eager faces turning.
    O captain! dear father!
    This arm ~~I push beneath you.~~ *beneath your head,*
    It is some dream that on the deck
      You've fallen cold and dead.

III.

My captain does not answer, his lips are pale and still:
My father does not feel my arm, he has no pulse nor will.
~~But the ship,~~ The ship is anchored safe, its voyage closed and done: *and sound.*
From fearful trip the victor ship comes in with object won!
    Exult, O shores! and ring, O bells!
    But I, with silent tread,
    Walk the spot my captain lies
      Fallen cold and dead.

WHITMAN'S TRIBUTE TO LINCOLN

Walt Whitman (1819–1892) wrote this dirge for the death of Abraham Lincoln in 1865. Published to immediate acclaim in the New York City *Saturday Press*, "O Captain! My Captain!" was widely anthologized during his lifetime. In the 1880s, when Whitman gave public lectures and readings, he was asked to recite the poem so often that he said: "I'm almost sorry I ever wrote [it]," though it had "certain emotional immediate reasons for being."

While Whitman is renowned as the most innovative of American poets, this poem is a rare example of his use of rhymed, rhythmically regular verse, which serves to create a somber yet exalted effect. Whitman had envisioned Lincoln as an archangel captain, and reportedly dreamed the night before the assassination about a ship entering harbor under full sail.

Restlessly creative, Whitman was still revising "O Captain! My Captain!" decades after its creation. Pictured here is a proof sheet of the poem, with his corrections, which was readied for publication in 1888. The editors apparently had erred by picking up earlier versions of punctuation and whole lines that had appeared in the poem prior to Whitman's 1871 revision. On the back is written:

Dear Sirs

Thank you for the little books, No. 32 "Riverside Literature Series"—Somehow you have got a couple of bad perversions in "O Captain," & I send you a corrected sheet—

Walt Whitman

The Library holds the world's largest collection of Walt Whitman materials, featuring more than twenty thousand manuscript items alone.

A DOLLAR BOOK FOR A DIME

With a June 1860 advertisement promising "BOOKS FOR THE MILLION! A Dollar Book for a Dime," Irwin P. Beadle & Company launched a publishing phenomenon that would provide average adult and adolescent readers with a wealth of popular fiction in a regular series at a fixed, inexpensive price. Beadle's Dime Novels, No. 1, *Malaeska; the Indian Wife of the White Hunter,* by Ann A. Stephens, appeared in a small booklet format with the later-to-be-standard orange wrapper. This story, which deals with the struggles of frontier life, had been published originally in *The Ladies Home Companion* more than twenty years earlier when the author was editor of that magazine. Irwin Beadle paid Stephens $250 for the privilege of reprinting her popular story. As the popularity of dime novels grew, Prentiss Ingrahm, the author of *The Texan Trailer*, became one of Beadle's most popular and prolific authors, often turning out two seventy-thousand-word novels a month (in longhand).

As was the case with *Malaeska*, the great majority of the early dime novels were truly American tales of the wilderness, many of them featuring encounters between Native Americans and backwoods settlers, and were fiercely nationalistic and patriotic. Attesting to the continuing popularity of these themes, seventeen titles were reissued in the 1870s as *Frank Starr's American Novels*. New topics and formats were introduced as publishers vied for a share of the burgeoning market. By the mid-1890s, the house of Beadle was fading, while competitor Street & Smith's bold color covers depicting scenes of bloodshed and courage captured the imaginations of a mostly adolescent audience.

Through copyright deposit the Library of Congress has accumulated a dime novel collection of nearly forty thousand titles representing nearly 280 of the approximately 360 series published between 1860 and 1933.

what made them; but Toto knew, and he walked close to Dorothy's side, and did not even bark in return.

"How long will it be," the child asked of the Tin Woodman, "before we are out of the forest?"

"I cannot tell," was the answer, "for I have never been to the Emerald City. But my father went there once, when I was a boy, and he said it was a long journey through a dangerous country, although nearer to the city where Oz dwells the country is beautiful. But I am not afraid so long as I have my oil-can, and nothing can hurt the Scarecrow, while you bear upon your forehead the mark of the good Witch's kiss, and that will protect you from harm."

"But Toto!" said the girl, anxiously; "what will protect him?"

"We must protect him ourselves, if he is in danger," replied the Tin Woodman.

Just as he spoke there came from the forest a terrible roar, and the next moment a great Lion bounded into the road. With one blow of his paw he sent the Scarecrow spining over and over to the edge of the road, and then he struck at the Tin Woodman with his sharp claws. But, to the Lion's surprise, he could make no impression on the tin, although the Woodman fell over in the road and lay still.

Little Toto, now that he had an enemy to face, ran barking toward the Lion, and the great beast had opened

" You ought to be ashamed of yourself!"

WE'RE OFF TO SEE THE WIZARD

The Wonderful Wizard of Oz, published in 1900, is the first American fairy tale and the first fantasy written by an American to enjoy an immediate success upon publication. So powerful was its effect on the American imagination, so evocative its use of the forces of nature in its plots, so charming its invitation to children of all ages to look for the element of wonder in the world around them that author L. Frank Baum was forced by demand to create book after book about Dorothy and her friends—including the Scarecrow, the Tin Woodman, the Cowardly Lion, and Glinda the Good Witch.

When Baum died in 1919, the series lived on under the authorship of Ruth Plumly Thompson and others who themselves had loved the stories as children. Published in many foreign countries, *The Wizard* even found its way as far as Russia, where it was translated in 1939 by Alexander Volkov, who then wrote two Oz books of his own. That was also the year that Dorothy and her friends appeared on the silver screen in the immortal MGM adaptation featuring Judy Garland, Ray Bolger, Jack Haley, and Bert Lahr.

This exquisite first edition, vibrantly illustrated by W. W. Denslow, was given to the Library in 1982 by antiquarian book dealer E. R. Meyer, in memory of his daughter, Margit.

SUPERMAN TO THE RESCUE

During the 1930s and 1940s, the Golden Age of comic books, the original comic book publishers introduced such well-known characters as Batman, Wonder Woman, and Captain America. But Superman remains the quintessential comic book hero in the popular mind—*almost* all-powerful and always the champion of the underdog. The cover of this 1945 Superman adventure reveals a "Supersecret" (that our hero is ticklish).

The Library of Congress acquires comic books through copyright deposit. The current collection of forty-eight hundred titles, probably the largest in the United States, contains approximately 100,000 issues, some dating back almost sixty years. Represented in the collection is the entire range of comic book subject matter: western, science fiction, detective, adventure, war, romance, horror, and humor.

Action Comics, *Archie*, *Detective Comics*, *Tarzan*, and *Wonder Woman* are among those titles for which the Library owns nearly complete runs. Because of the rapid deterioration of the paper and the value of older issues, full access to the comic book collection is restricted to readers engaged in serious research.

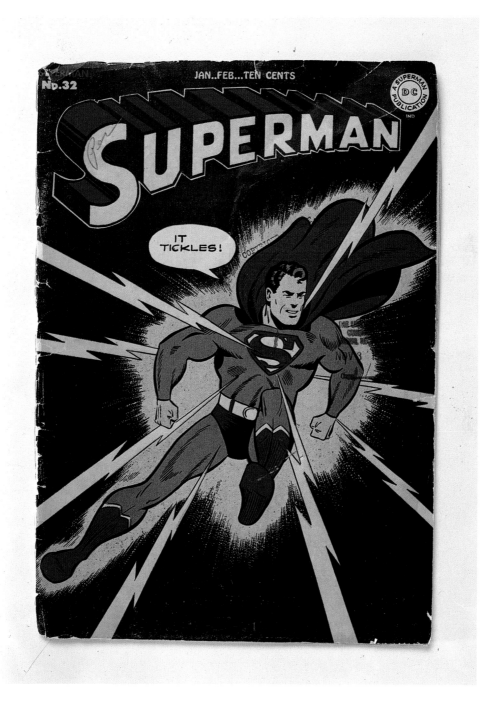

For Stewart from Robert
On the Day Jan 20 1961

DEDICATION

Summoning
~~artists~~ artists to participate

In the august occasions of the state

Seems something for us all to celebrate.

This day is for my cause a day of days,

And his be poetry's old-fashioned praise

Who was the first to think of such a thing.

This tibute verse to be his own,I bring

Is about the new order of the ages

That *in* the Latin of the founding sages

God nodded His approval of as good.

So much those sages knew and understood

I The mighty four of them were Washington,

John Adams, Jefferson, and Madison)—

So much they saw as consecrated seers

They must have seen how in two hundred years

2.

They would bring down the world about our ears

By the example of our Declaration,

It made
~~Made~~ the least tribe want to be a nation.

New order of the ages did they say ?

The newest thing in which they led the way

Is in our very papers of the day.

Colonial had been the thing to be

As long as the great issue was to see

Which country be the one to dominate

By character, by tongue, and native ~~trait~~ trait

England   *first had*
What Christopher Columbus' ~~~~ found.

The French, the Spanish, and the Dutch were downed,

was
They all were counted out: the deed was done:

Elizabeth the first and England won.

Of what had been for centuries the trend

This turned out the beginning of the end.

My verse purports to be the guiding #### chart

~~~~was ours to start.
To the centenary it was time to start

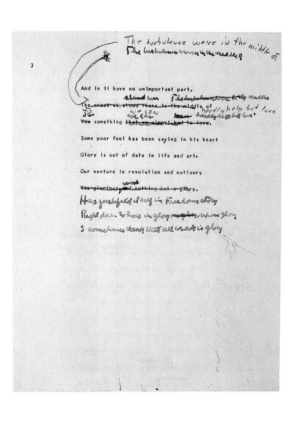

The turbulence we're in the middle of
~~The turbulence we're in the middle~~

3

And in it have no unimportant part.

~~The wreck we stood there in the middle~~   *hardly help but love*

~~Was something that so almost but to love.~~   *hardly help but love*

Some poor fool has been saying in his heart

Glory is out of date in life and art.

Our venture in revolution and outlawry

~~Was glorious and nothing but a glory.~~

Has justified itself in Freedoms story

Right does. so does in glory, whose glory

I sometimes think that all work is glory

"SUMMONING ARTISTS TO PARTICIPATE IN THE AUGUST OCCASIONS OF THE STATE . . ."

Poet Robert Frost (1874–1963) composed "Dedication" for delivery at the inauguration of President John F. Kennedy on January 20, 1961, and intended to read it from the text shown here. He was unable to read, however, because of the glare of the sun upon snow. Instead, the poet put the manuscript aside and recited his poem "The Gift Outright" from memory.

This first version of "Dedication" was donated to the Library in 1969 by Stewart L. Udall, who was secretary of the interior in the Kennedy cabinet. Udall explained that no one had expected Frost to write a new poem for the inauguration as "he had steadfastly refused to compose commemorative verses during his entire lifetime." Udall had heard Frost reciting the poem before the ceremony and after the event asked the poet for the original manuscript of the unread composition. Frost agreed and added the inscription above the title: "For Stewart from Robert on the Day, Jan 20 1961."

Frost's associations with the Library of Congress encompass more than manuscripts and volumes of his published poems. He served as the Library's Consultant in Poetry (1958–59) and as Honorary Consultant in the Humanities (1958–63). In the photograph reproduced here he is seen in a Library recording studio on one of the several occasions he recorded his poetry for the Library's Archive of Recorded Poetry and Literature.

GORDON PARKS AND *THE LEARNING TREE*

Besides *The Wizard of Oz* (MGM, 1939), can you name another American movie set in Kansas in which the leading character encounters a tornado in the first reel? The answer is Gordon Parks's *The Learning Tree* (Warner Bros., 1969).

In 1969 Parks unified his many artistic talents by writing, producing, directing, and composing the musical score for this semiautobiographical theatrical feature motion picture. It is based on his 1963 novel of the same name, about the life and education of an African-American teenager in 1920s Kansas. In 1989 *The Learning Tree* was among the first twenty-five films selected for the Library of Congress National Film Preservation Registry in recognition of its contribution to the history of American cinema. Apart from its considerable aesthetic achievements in direction, writing, and Cinemascope cinematography, *The Learning Tree* is also historically important for being the first general release motion picture by an African-American director/producer to be financed by a major American studio.

The manuscript of the novel *The Learning Tree,* displayed here with a frame enlargement from the film, is from the Gordon Parks Collection, which Parks donated to the Library of Congress in 1995, adding to the many photographic negatives he created for the Farm Security Administration (FSA) already in the Library's holdings. Among the items in his archives are thousands of photographs, films, audiotapes, videos, manuscripts, letters, and other ephemera relating to the many creative endeavors undertaken by Parks during his career.

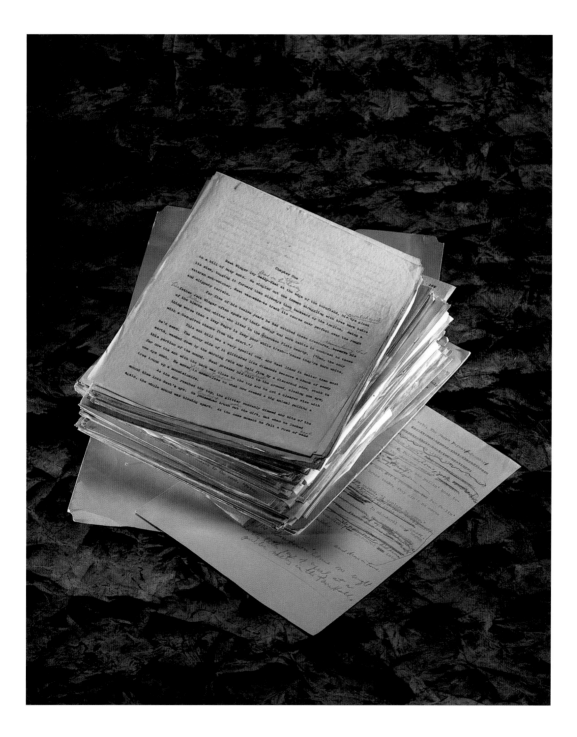

THE ART OF THE BOOK

Night Street, featuring the poetry of Barbara Luck and illustrated by Lois Johnson, is a book in which the design truly bears the influence of the content. Published by the Janus Press, a small but important printing venture, the book is an example of the creativity of the small press movement in America—a movement devoted to the book as a product of collaborative and intensely aesthetic energies on the part of several artists and craftsmen, whether they be artisans of the word, of the visual image, or of the printed and bound page. The Janus Press was founded by Claire Van Vliet in 1955, and with unflagging energy she has run the press for more than forty years. The Library has collected her work from the press's inception, and recently it received the entire Janus Press archives, comprising drawings, proofs, layouts, and designs for each book Van Vliet has produced. The press strives for a balance between various claims to attention and affection that a book exerts upon the reader/viewer/handler.

The Rare Book and Special Collections Division of the Library of Congress has long collected premier examples of the book arts, from the Middle Ages to the present, and is the repository of the collections of the early-twentieth-century book designers Frederic Goudy and Bruce Rogers, as well as contemporaries of Van Vliet such as Leonard Baskin of Gehenna Press and Timothy Ely.

THOMAS JEFFERSON'S "MACCARONI" MACHINE

Thomas Jefferson noted these plans for a macaroni or pasta machine while touring northern Italy in 1787. When Jefferson prepared these plans, macaroni was a highly fashionable food in Paris, where he was stationed as ambassador to France. He later commissioned his secretary William Short to purchase a macaroni machine in Italy, but the machine was not very durable. In later years Jefferson served macaroni or spaghetti made by cutting rolled dough into strips, which were then rolled by hand into noodles. While in France, Jefferson became enamored with French *cuisine bourgeoise,* and not only had his slave, James Heming, trained as a cook, but later brought his French butler, Adrien Petit, to the United States. Jefferson acquired a stock of standard French recipes for French fries, sauces, fruit tarts, desserts, blood sausages, pigs' feet, rabbits, and pigeons, which he served to his guests at Monticello.

CHAMPIONS OF AMERICA.

Entered according to Act of Congress, in the year 1865, by Chas. H. Williamson, in the Clerk's Office of the District Court of the United States, of the Eastern District of New York.

THE '65 BROOKLYN ATLANTICS

Baseball, America's national pastime, evolved from a child's game to an organized sport in the 1840s and 1850s. It was an urban sport, and the first teams were established in New York City and Brooklyn. By 1860 baseball had replaced cricket as the nation's most popular ball game. Before the Civil War, more than one hundred baseball teams played in the New York City area. During the war, the number of teams dwindled to less than thirty, but thousands of spectators flocked to games.

The Brooklyn Atlantics dominated early baseball by winning championships in 1861, 1864, and 1865. The Atlantics usually crushed their competition, scoring two or three times more runs than their opponents. It was an amateur sport: according to the rules of the National Association of Base Ball Players, athletes could not accept wages to play ball, though gifts and jobs were sometimes offered as a means of compensation.

Baseball cards as we know them did not become commonplace until the 1880s. This early prototype is actually an original photograph mounted on a card. At the start of the 1865 season, the Atlantics presented opposing teams with these framed photographs of the "Champion Nine." The Scottish-born photographer, Charles H. Williamson, opened a daguerreotype studio in Brooklyn in 1851, continuing to work as a photographer until his death in 1874.

THE FASHIONS OF THE CUISINE

As the editor of Marie Martinelo's 1882 *The New York Cook Book* reminds us, "The fashions of the *cuisine*, like those of the dress, are subject to changes." Nowhere is that so clear as in the Library's incomparable collection of cookbooks, including the many cookbooks in the General Collections, and, in the Rare Book and Special Collections Division, the Elizabeth Pennell Collection and the 4,346-volume Katherine Golden Bitting Collection, donated by Bitting's husband.

Katherine Bitting, a food chemist with the Department of Agriculture and herself the author of numerous books and pamphlets about food preservation and consumption, acquired Martinelo's "complete manual of cookery in all its branches." In addition to recipes, the book includes helpful household hints on such things as making one's own soap and ink; how to eradicate "household vermin" like ants and spiders with a mixture of hellebore and molasses; how to remove rust from cutlery (in the days before stainless steel); and how to prepare special dishes for the infirm such as tapioca jelly and wine possets. Appended to this volume is a special treat: "Miss Leslie's seventy-five receipts for pastry, cakes and sweetmeats," temptingly illustrated with this chromolithograph of various fashionable desserts that once were common but are now seldom prepared at home by those who are health-conscious and/or pressed for time. *The New York Cook Book* is one of a number of such volumes at the Library that have been consulted by, among others, film art directors trying to create an authentic period feel in their productions.

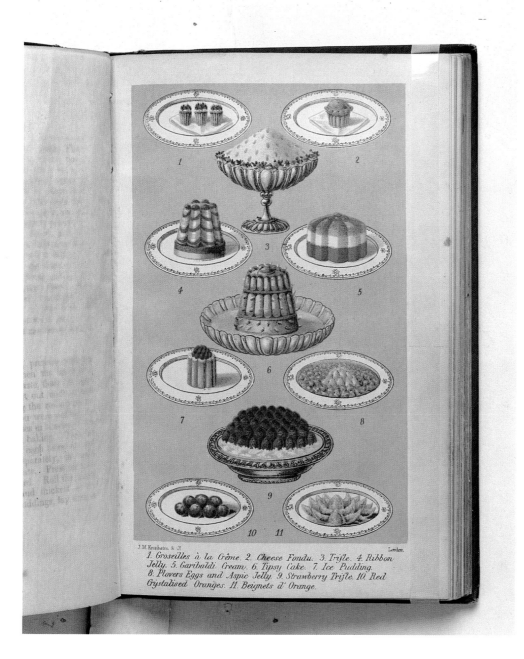

J.M. Kronheim. & C?   London.

1. *Groseilles à la Crême. 2. Cheese Fondu. 3. Trifle. 4. Ribbon Jelly. 5. Garibaldi Cream. 6. Tipsy Cake. 7. Ice Pudding. 8. Plovers Eggs and Aspic Jelly. 9. Strawberry Trifle. 10. Red Crystalised Oranges. 11. Beignets d' Orange.*

THE GREAT HOUDINI

Harry Houdini (1874–1926), the legendary king of escape and folk hero of magic enthusiasts, claimed Appleton, Wisconsin, as home, even though he was born in Budapest, Hungary, with the given name Ehrich Weiss. Since Houdini's rabbi father had lost his position before Ehrich was ten, the boy began earning money to help support his family by performing as a contortionist and trapeze artist in a local circus. Greatly influenced by the autobiography of the French magician Robert-Houdin, by age fourteen Ehrich decided to be "like Houdin." Adopting the name "Houdini," he became a brilliant escape artist and showman.

This dramatic portrait of Houdini is included in a scrapbook of highlights of the magician's exceptional career. It is part of the McManus-Young Collection of magica, given to the Library in 1955, a rich collection of rare books, pamphlets, magazines, clipping files, scrapbooks, and magical apparatuses. The Library also holds a separate Houdini Collection, materials received in 1927 through Houdini's bequest and predominantly comprising works on spiritualism and psychic phenomena that Houdini assembled to expose the false claims of fake spirit mediums. Houdini's library includes several significant books on the history of magic, as well as about fifty scrapbooks Houdini compiled or acquired from other figures in magic. Other scrapbooks illustrate the wide range of Houdini's interests, including music, drama, politics, and literature.

ENDLESS SUMMER

In July 1957, Toni Frissell (1907–1988) made this photograph as part of a *Sports Illustrated* picture story about a group of families who vacationed together each year at the Thousand Islands, a large group of islands in the St. Lawrence River, located in a widening of the river between New York State and Ontario. For seventy-five years a half-dozen families from various U.S. cities and Europe came together to "the River" to fish, row and sail skiffs unique to the region, and carry on intense three-generational tennis matches and baseball games. Over the years, a dozen marriages resulted from the summer meetings of the clans.

Frissell herself joined the tradition when she married into the Bacon family. She had already started making a name for herself as a photographer when she married New York society member Francis Bacon, so she continued her career under her maiden name. She worked on the staffs of *Vogue* and *Harper's Bazaar* and sold stories independently to other top magazines, as well as making two trips to photograph World War II in the European theater.

Always the sports enthusiast, Frissell found a way to put her athleticism to professional advantage in 1953 by becoming the first female on the staff of the recently begun *Sports Illustrated*. A female sports photographer was a rarity at the time. When the Baltimore Museum of Art mounted its *Man in Sport* exhibition in 1968, Frissell was the only woman in a long list of photographers selected for the show.

BUILDING THE NATIONAL COLLECTION

In 1800, as the American government prepared to move from its temporary headquarters in Philadelphia to its permanent (and as yet unbuilt) home on the Potomac River, one of its first acts was to appropriate $5,000 "for the purchase of such books as may be necessary for the use of Congress . . . and for fitting up a suitable apartment for containing them and for placing them therein." In the same omnibus bill, "An Act to make provision for the removal and accommodation of the Government," Congress also set aside $10,000 to pave the sidewalks in the notoriously swampy land of Washington, D.C. But the appropriation of such a large sum for books, when members of Congress had trouble negotiating the muddy streets on the way to work every day, indicates that from the beginning, American statesmen have viewed a library not as a luxury, but as an essential working tool for the creation and maintenance of a healthy democracy. Soon thereafter, borrowing privileges for the congressional library were extended to the president and his cabinet, as well as to the Supreme Court, which was located, like the library itself, in the Capitol. After the British invaded Washington during the War of 1812 and torched the Capitol, fueling the flames with books pulled from library shelves, Congress took immediate steps to replenish its bookshelves. Members paid Thomas Jefferson, then living in retirement in Monticello, $23,950 for the nearly sixty-five hundred books he offered them. That was almost twice the number of titles lost in the conflagration. The universal scope of subject matter, as well as the variety of formats and languages in the Jefferson library set the Library of Congress standards for collecting for the centuries ahead.

Since 1800 the congressional appropriation for purchase of books and other Library items has grown from $5,000 to $8 million, but that amount is only a small fraction of the worth of the Library's acquisitions every year. What had been a slow but steady growth of the collections in the nineteenth century exploded exponentially in 1870, the year that the Copyright Office became a part of the Library of Congress. From then on, all creators wishing to protect their intellectual property rights by registering their work with the office were required to deposit a copy of that work in the Library. It is the cumulative record of copyright deposits that has so profoundly shaped the nature of the collection at the Library of Congress and transformed the congressional library into the memory bank of the nation. For it is not only writers who register for copyright, but composers, engravers, cartoonists, mapmakers, photographers, filmmakers, recording artists, poster designers, architects, engineers, speech-writers, television scriptwriters, advertising artists, comic book publishers, software writers, and many others, who have, over the decades, added to the Library's record of American creativity. Because of the careful preservation of copyright deposits at the Library, researchers now have access to unique items such as a collection of the earliest known motion pictures—including Fred Ott's sneeze—and a number of the oldest baseball cards.

Donation is another invaluable source of the collections, especially in the area of personal papers and rare items. Often prominent Americans, such as Groucho Marx, Gordon Parks, or Toni Frissell, make a provision to leave their papers to the Library before or after their deaths. In other cases, the heirs of such people as Abraham Lincoln, Orville Wright, and Leonard Bernstein place their papers here to make them available to the widest possible audience and to have them preserved for future generations. The Library also receives a significant amount of material through transfers from other institutions. The papers of Washington, Jefferson, Madison, Monroe, Franklin, and Hamilton were transferred by the State Department to the Library in 1903. Many maps come to the Library this way, for most maps are created by government agencies. We also acquired the Federal Theatre Project Archives and the Farm Security Administration photographs, two of our most heavily used collections, by transfer.

In 1815, the year that Jefferson sold his library to Congress, he confided to his friend John Adams, "I cannot live without books" and began to amass another personal library. If he were alive today, he would no doubt collect in all the new formats that have appeared since his time—audio recordings, films, photographs, CD-ROMS. While the Library does not keep a copy of every book printed in the United States (no library is that comprehensive!), or acquire the papers of every distinguished American, it does have the best and most comprehensive collection of Americana in the world. It is here that the nation's great experiment in democracy is recorded and here that this generation and future generations can learn for themselves who they are and where they came from.

ABBY SMITH
EXHIBIT CURATOR

PRESERVING THE PAST

Every time the Library acquires an item, it makes a commitment both to preserve and to make accessible the information that item contains as long as possible so that it might be used not only by the present generation but by future generations as well. The task of preservation is to insure that our documentary heritage remains available for use over an extended period without losing the information and essence that make it important to American culture.

The Library's diverse collections comprise almost all forms devised by humanity to record information. They range from books, manuscripts, maps, and works of art on paper; to motion picture film, videotape, and photographic materials; to phonograph records, tape recordings, cylinder discs, and compact discs. They also encompass a surprising variety of objects, including flutes, globes, gramophones, microphones, and even the contents of Lincoln's pockets on the night he was assassinated.

The Library's strategy for preserving its vast collections reflects this diversity. Different materials age in different ways, and every item in the collection has its own particular preservation needs. Library materials are primarily organic in nature and, like other living things, will eventually deteriorate. Expressed simply, our preservation strategy is to practice preventive maintenance in order to avoid costly treatments in the future. Thus, the Library's preservation program comprises a holistic array of options intended to keep the collections in a stable state so that they can be maintained in a usable condition for as long as possible. Environmental control, appropriate housing and storage, and careful handling are the first line of defense against inherent degradation.

In certain cases, a delicate balance must be reached between preservation and access, between making an item available for researchers today and risking dramatically shortening the length of its use by future researchers. In the case of newspapers from the turn of the century printed on brittle, highly acidic paper that crumbles with handling, the Library makes the information contained in the item available by creating a surrogate image—in this case, microfilm or microfiche. In such a case, where one can possibly destroy the item by using it, the choice is clear—preservation of the information is more important than preservation of the object itself.

But what about rare and fragile documents that have special significance to the nation not only for the information they contain, but also as artifacts—such as autograph (handwritten) items by Washington, Jefferson, or Lincoln? A special strategy must be worked out to make these documents available in the original form to the public, while at the same time to extend the life of these precious items particularly at risk. The Library has placed treasures such as the Gettysburg Address in specially built environmental containers in which the oxygen has been expelled and replaced with the inert gas argon. The cases prevent oxidation, including photooxidation, and are covered with double ultraviolet-light acrylic glazing to enable safe display under low light conditions. These containers are in turn stored in a low-temperature vault that is maintained at a constant environmental level of fifty degrees Fahrenheit and 50 percent relative humidity. The vault has a fire-suppression system and is maintained under high security protocols.

In certain special cases, preventive maintenance is not enough because the document has already suffered serious deterioration. When conservation work began on George Washington's map of Alexandria, which he made in 1749 when he was seventeen, the conservator had to address a number of different problems. For example, the map's paper was torn along every fold line, it was worn thin in many places, and the ink was flaking off.

The Library of Congress conservator began by stabilizing the ink with a consolidant to prevent further loss. While peering through a microscope, working at a painstakingly slow pace, she proceeded to remove the paper lining by wetting discrete portions at a time in order to soften the lining and adhesive enough to scrape it away. At the same time, every precaution was taken to keep the map and ink as dry as possible. Once the linings were removed, the tears were meticulously mended with the thinnest strips of Japanese tissue and the losses filled with eighteenth-century handmade laid paper. The conservator took great care that the treatment would in no way further damage the map or prove to be irreversible in the future.

While the dawning age of digital images holds the promise of making the Library's collections ever more widely available to users, the challenge of preserving the cultural heritage that the Library holds in trust for the American people continues to grow, as more and more of what the

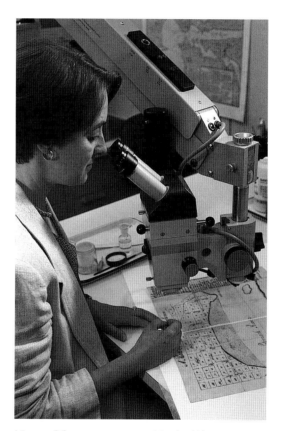

Library of Congress conservator Heather Wanser treats George Washington's 1749 map of Alexandria

nation produces is on highly unstable new media, such as video- and audiotape. The Library's in-house preservation research and development facilities are busy addressing these challenges and trying to anticipate new ones as the creators of our generation are busy inventing the future.

The items featured in this volume are a small but representative selection from the Library's rich holdings of Americana. In making this selection, the curatorial staff had a difficult task, given how large and significant the collections are. There is simply no way to include everything that is important and truly treasured in the Library. We have tried to give a sense of the depth, breadth, and variety of the holdings, as well as represent in some fashion the most important and often most heavily used collections. Beyond that, we have also selected items that we hope will convey to the reader the sense of surprise, discovery, and serendipity that each day attends the curators and researchers who work with the Library's collections—the unpublished version of a well-known work, the unfinished or unrealized dream of a restless mind, the false starts and bitter failures that are intrinsic parts of the creative process.

A number of the Library's curatorial staff contributed time and text to this volume. They are listed, with gratitude, below. Their initials also appear in the object list that follows, at the end of the descriptions of the items for which they contributed text.

Alice Birney (AB), Manuscript Division; Beverly W. Brannan (BWB), Prints and Photographs Division; Leonard C. Bruno (LB), Manuscript Division; Samuel Brylawski (SB), Motion Picture, Broadcasting and Recorded Sound Division; Verna P. Curtis (VPC), Prints and Photographs Division; Donald R. DeGlopper (DD), Law Library; Gerard W. Gawalt (GWG), Manuscript Division; Judith A. Gray (JAG), American Folklife Center; Ronald E. Grim (REG), Geography and Map Division; Michael Grunberger (MG), Hebraic Section; John E. Haynes (JEH), Manuscript Division; Sybille Jagusch (SJ), Children's Literature Center; Carol Johnson (CJ), Prints and Photographs Division; Harry L. Katz (HLK), Prints and Photographs Division; Marvin W. Kranz (MWK), Manuscript Division; Patrick G. Loughney (PGL), Motion Picture, Broadcasting and Recorded Sound Division; John McDonough (JM), Manuscript Division; Elena Millie (EM), Prints and Photographs Division; Lyle W. Minter (LWM), Serial and Government Publications Division; Thomas Noonan (TN), Rare Book and Special Collections Division; C. Ford Peatross (CFP), Prints and Photographs Division; Rosemary Fry Plakas (RFP), Rare Book and Special Collections Division; John R. Sellers (JRS), Manuscript Division; Robert Sheldon (RS), Music Division; Wayne Shirley (WS), Music Division; Abby Smith (AS), Library Services; Merrily A. Smith (MAS), Preservation; Heather Wanser (HW), Preservation; Raymond A. White (RAW), Music Division; David Wigdor (DW), Manuscript Division; Patricia Willard (PW), Music Division; Walter W. Zvonchenko (WZ), Music Division

MEMORY

1. Biblia. Old Testament. Psalms. *The Whole Booke of Psalmes Faithfully Translated into English Metre.* Cambridge, Mass.: 1640. American Imprint Collection, 1640, Rare Book and Special Collections Division. Gift, 1966. (RFP, AS)

2. *Die bittre Gute, oder Das Gesang der einsamen Turtel-Taube, der christlichen Kirche hier auf Erden, die annoch im Trauerthal auf dem dürren Aesten und Zweigen den Stand ihrer Wittwenschaft beklagt, und dabey in Hoffnung singt von einer andern und nochmaligen Vermählung.* Ephrata, Pa.: 1746. Music Division. Purchased at auction, 1927. (WS)

3. Anonymous. Powder horn inscribed with map of Hudson and Mohawk River Valleys. Cow or ox horn, polished and finely engraved, 1757–60. Powder Horn Collection, Geography and Map Division. Purchase, 1867. (REG)

4. Briton Hammon (fl. 1760). *A narrative of the uncommon sufferings, and surprizing deliverance of Briton Hammon, a negro man,—servant to General Winslow, of Marshfield, in New-England; who returned to Boston, after having been absent almost thirteen years.* Printed and sold in Boston by Green &

Russell, 1760. 14 p. American Imprint Collection, 1760, Rare Book and Special Collections Division. Purchase. (RFP)

5. Commission of General George Washington, 19 June 1775. Holograph manuscript on vellum. George Washington Papers, Manuscript Division. (GWG)

6. Moses Seixas (1744–1809). "Congratulatory Address to George Washington on Behalf of the Hebrew Congregation of Newport, Rhode Island," 17 August 1790. George Washington Papers, Manuscript Division. (MG)

7. H. C. Howard, printers, Philadelphia. "For President ABRAM LINCOLN. For Vice President HANNIBAL HAMLIN." Woodcut or lithograph, 1860. Prints and Photographs Division. Deposited for Copyright, 1860. (HLK)

8. Abraham Lincoln (1809–1865). First Inaugural Address, 4 March 1861. Robert Todd Lincoln Papers, Manuscript Division. (JRS)

9. Alfred Waud (1828–1891). *Custer's Division Retiring from Mount Jackson in the Shenandoah Valley, October 7, 1864*. Pencil and opaque white on tan paper, 1864. Prints and Photographs Division. Gift, J. P. Morgan, 1919. (HLK)

10. Contents of President Abraham Lincoln's pockets on the night of his assassination (bequest of Mary Lincoln Isham); *The New York Times*, 15 April 1865, vol. XIV, no. 4236, showing the announcement of Lincoln's death (gift of Alfred Whital Stern). Rare Book and Special Collections Division. (JRS, RFP)

11. *Tombstone, Arizona.* New York: Sanborn Map and Publishing Company, 1886. Color printed map. Sanborn Map Collection, Geography and Map Division. (REG)

12. Wax cylinder recordings of Passamaquoddy songs and stories, March 1890. Jesse Walter Fewkes Collection, Archive of Folk Culture, American Folklife Center. Shown with Columbia Graphophone, Model N. Motion Picture, Broadcasting and Recorded Sound Division. (JAG)

13. Theodore Roosevelt, Sr. (1858–1919), to Theodore Roosevelt, Jr. (1887–1944), 11 July 1890. Handwritten letter on U.S. Civil Service Commission stationery. Theodore Roosevelt, Jr. Papers, Manuscript Division. (JEH)

14. James Montgomery Flagg (1877–1960). *I Want You For U.S. Army.* Lithograph, 1917. Prints and Photographs Division. (EM)

15. Dorothea Lange (1895–1965). "On these workers the crops of California depend—Brushing tomato plants near Indio, March 1, 1935" in *Establishment of rural rehabilitation camps for migrants in California*, 15 March 1935; "More Oklahomans reach Calif. via the cotton fields of Ariz.," "We got blowed out in Oklahoma," and "Share-croppers family near Bakersfield Apr. 7-1935" in *Migration of Drought Refugees to California*, 17 April 1935. Gelatin silver prints. Prints and Photographs Division. (BWB, CJ)

16. Orson Welles (1915–1985). Costume design for Cardinal of Lorraine. Textile swatches and mixed drawing mediums. For the stage production, *The Tragical History of Doctor Faustus* by Christopher Marlowe; Maxine Elliott's Theatre, New York City, 8 January 1937. Federal Theatre Project Archives, Music Division. (WZ)

17. Irving Berlin (1888–1989). "God Bless America." Manuscripts and proof sheets. Irving Berlin Collection, Music Division. (RAW)

18. NBC master program book and index card from Program Analysis File: World War II programs; shown with 1938 microphone. Motion Picture, Broadcasting and Recorded Sound Division. (SB)

19. Soviet Premier Joseph Stalin (1879–1953) to W. Averell Harriman (1891–1986), 13 August 1942, Moscow. Memorandum in Russian signed by Joseph Stalin. W. Averell Harriman Papers, Manuscript Division. (JEH)

20. *The Tonight Show* (NBC-TV); telecast, 5 October 1965. Starring Johnny Carson and Groucho Marx. Motion Picture, Broadcasting and Recorded Sound Division. Gift of NBC. (PGL)

21. Maya Ying Lin (b. 1959). Vietnam Veterans Memorial Competition. Presentation panel in mixed mediums on paper, 1981. ADE Unit 2228, no. 1, E Size. Architecture, Design and Engineering Collections, Prints and Photographs Division. Gift, 1985. (CFP)

REASON

22. *The Book of the General Laws of the Inhabitants of the Jurisdiction of New-Plimouth, Collected out of the Records of the General Court, And lately Revised: And with some Emendations and Additions Established and Disposed into such Order as they may readily Conduce to General Use and Benefit.* Boston: Samuel Green, 1685. Rare Book Room, Law Library. (DD)

23. Virginia Declaration of Rights. 1776. Holograph Manuscript in the hand of George Mason and Thomas Ludwell Lee (beginning with the phrase "That the freedom of the press"). George Mason Papers, Manuscript Division. (GWG)

24. First page of the "Rough Draught" of the Declaration of Independence. 1776. Holograph in the hand of Thomas Jefferson with minor emendations in the hands of John

Adams and Benjamin Franklin. Thomas Jefferson Papers, Manuscript Division. (GWG)

25. Broadside. *In Congress, July 4, 1776, A Declaration By the Representatives of the United States of America, In General Congress Assembled.* Philadelphia: John Dunlap, 4 July 1776. Shown with letter of 6 July 1776 from John Hancock, president of the Continental Congress. George Washington Papers, Manuscript Division. (GWG)

26. Matthew Wheelock, *Reflections moral and political on Great Britain and her colonies.* London, 1770. 66 p.; bound with Allan Ramsay, *Thoughts on the origin and nature of government. Occasioned by the late disputes between Great Britain and her American colonies.* London, 1769. 64 p. Colonial Pamphlets, v. 26. Jefferson Collection, Rare Book and Special Collections Division. (AS)

27. *The Slavery Code of the District of Columbia together with Notes and Judicial Decisions Explanatory of the Same.* By a Member of the Washington Bar. Washington, D.C.: L. Towers, 1862; and *Slavery Code of the District of Columbia.* Manuscript, 1860. Rare Book Room, Law Library. (DD)

28. Abraham Lincoln. First sketch of the Emancipation Proclamation. July 1862. Abraham Lincoln Papers, Manuscript Division. (JRS)

29. Abraham Lincoln. First and second drafts of the Gettysburg Address. 1864. Abraham Lincoln Papers, Manuscript Division. (JRS)

30. *An Account of the Proceedings on the Trial of Susan B. Anthony, on the charge of illegal voting, at the presidential election in November 1872, and on the trial of Beverly W. Jones, Edwin T. Marsh, and William B. Hall, the inspectors of election by whom her vote was received.* Rochester, N.Y.: 1874. vii, 212 p., 23 cm. Susan B. Anthony Collection, JK 1899, A6A5, Rare Book and Special Collections Division. (RFP)

31. Elihu Vedder (1836–1923). Maquette drawings for "Peace and Prosperity" and "Anarchy." Studies for Library of Congress Jefferson Building murals. Pastel on paper, c. 1896. Prints and Photographs Division. (HLK)

32. Billy (William H.) Gobitas (1925–1989) to School Directors, Minersville, Pennsylvania, 5 November 1935. Handwritten letter. William H. Gobitas Papers, Manuscript Division. (JEH)

33. Justice Felix Frankfurter (1882–1965). Draft decree regarding *Brown v. Board of Education of Topeka.* 8 April 1955. Felix Frankfurter Papers, Manuscript Division. (DW)

34. Paul Conrad (b. 1924). *Thurgood Marshall (1908–1993).* Ink on paper, 1993. Prints and Photographs Division. Gift of the artist, 1994. (HLK)

35. Thomas Say (1787–1834). *American Entomology: or Descriptions of the Insects of North America.* Philadelphia, 1824–28. 3 vol. QL 466 S27. Smithsonian Deposit. Rare Book and Special Collections Division. (AS)

36. Robert Cornelius (1809–1893). *Self-Portrait.* Quarter-plate daguerreotype, 1839. Prints and Photographs Division. Gift, 1996. (CJ)

37. Alexander Graham Bell (1847–1922). Notebook entry, 10 March 1876. Alexander Graham Bell Family Papers, Manuscript Division. (LB)

38. Emile Berliner (1851–1929). Gramophone (Isabelle Sayers Collection of Phonographic Materials); and January 1895 List of Plates (Robert Sanders Collection). Motion Picture, Broadcasting, and Recorded Sound Division. (SB)

39. *Edison Kinetoscopic Record of a Sneeze.* Copyright by W. K. L. Dickson for the Edison Film Manufacturing Company, 9 January 1894. Prints and Photographs Division. (PGL)

40. John T. Daniels (fl. 1900s). "First Flight," 17 December 1903. Orville Wright at controls. Distance: 120 feet; time: 12 seconds. Modern gelatin silver print from glass negative. Prints and Photographs Division. (LB, BWB)

41. Samuel de Champlain (1567–1635). *Description des costs, pts., rades, illes de la Nouuele France faict selon son vray me ridien. . . .* Manuscript chart on vellum, 1607. Vellum Chart Collection no. 15, Geography and Map Division. (REG)

42. George Washington (1732–1799). *A Plan of Alexandria, now Belhaven.* Manuscript map on paper, 1749. G3884. A3G46 1749 .W3 Vault, Geography and Map Division. (REG)

43. Pierre-Charles L'Enfant (1754–1825). *Plan of the city intended for the permanent seat of the government of t[he] United States: projected agreeable to the direction of the President of the United States, in pursuance of an act of Congress, passed on the sixteenth day of July, MDCCXC, establishing the permanent seat on the bank of the Potowmac.* Manuscript map on paper, 1791. G3850 1791 .L4, Geography and Map Division. (REG)

44. Nicholas King (1771–1812) with annotations by Meriwether Lewis (1774–1809). Map of Western North America. Manuscript map on paper, 1803. Lewis and Clark Collection A. Geography and Map Division. (REG)

45. James Wilson (1763–1855). *A New American Terrestrial Globe on which the Principal Places of the Known World are Accurately laid down, with the traced attempts of Captain Cook to discover a Southern Continent* (Bradford, Vt.: J. Wilson, 1811), hand-colored globe, 13 inches in diameter; *Three Inch Terrestrial Globe* (Albany, N.Y.: Wilson and Sons, 1820s), hand-

colored globe, 3 inches in diameter; and *A Celestial Globe with all the stars of the 1st, 2d, & 3d Magnitudes* (Albany, N.Y.: Wilson and Sons, 1820s), hand-colored globe, 3 inches in diameter. Globe Collection, Geography and Map Division. (REG)

46. Manuscript map, probably made by a French voyageur, with annotations by Henry Rowe Schoolcraft (1793–1864). c. 1831. 33.5 × 40.5 cm. Henry Rowe Schoolcraft Papers, Manuscript Division. (JM)

47. Jedediah Hotchkiss (1828–1899). *Sketch book of Jed. Hotchkiss, Capt. & Top. Eng. Hd. Qurs. 2nd Corps, Army of N. Virginia,* manuscript notebook, 1862–65; *Sketch book showing positions of Second Corps, A.N.Va. in engagements of 1864–5 by Jed. Hotchkiss, Top. Eng. 2nd Corps,* manuscript notebook, 1864–65; and "Map showing routes and camps of the Army of the Valley Dist. from Staunton, Va. to Washington, D.C. and back to Strasburg, Va. from June 27th to July 22nd 1864 to accompany the report of Jed. Hotchkiss, Top. Eng. V.D.," map no. 11 in "Report of the camps, marches and engagements, of the Second Corps, A.N.V. and of the Army of the Valley Dist., of the Department of Northern Virginia; during the Campaign of 1864; illustrated by maps & sketches, by Jed. Hotchkiss, Top. Eng. V.D.," manuscript atlas, 1864–65. Hotchkiss Map Collection, Geography and Map Division. (REG)

48. Timothy O'Sullivan (1840–1882). *Black Cañon Looking Above from Camp 8, Colorado River, Arizona 1871.* Albumen silver print, 1871. Prints and Photographs Division. Transfer, Department of War, Corps of Engineers. (CJ)

49. Hal Shelton (b. 1916). *Arizona.* Acrylic on zinc, 1955. The H. M. Gousha Company Collection, Geography and Map Division. (REG)

IMAGINATION

50. Stephen Hallet (1755–1825). United States Capitol Competition. Scheme E (Final). Sectional elevation showing the Conference Room. Ink and watercolor on paper, 1793. Prints and Photographs Division. Purchase, 1976. (CFP)

51. John Rubens Smith (1775–1849). *West Front of the United States Capitol.* Watercolor, c. 1830. Prints and Photographs Division. Gift of Marian S. Carson and the James Madison Council, 1993. (HLK)

52. Richard Upjohn (1802–1878). Unidentified Gothic Revival Church. Elevations and details. Graphite, ink, and watercolor

on paper, c. 1850s. Prints and Photographs Division. Purchase and Gift of Melvin A. Brosterman and the James Madison Council, 1995–96. (CFP)

53. Frank Lloyd Wright (1867–1959). Dr. John Storer House, Hollywood, California. Perspective. Graphite and colored pencil on paper, 1923. Architecture, Design and Engineering Collections, Prints and Photographs Division. Gift, 1989. (CFP)

54. John Philip Sousa (1854–1932). "The Stars and Stripes Forever March." Holograph full score for band in ink; 8 leaves. At end: "John Philip Sousa. April 26, 1897. Boston, Mass." Music Division. Gift of the Sousa Family. (RAW)

55. Native American flutes: (top) Flute #480 (with stylized animal flute cover), obtained from Red Fox, a Quapaw of Miami, Oklahoma, in 1925, and given to the Library by Thurlow Lieutance; (middle) Flute #205 (with lead insets), made by Henry Johnson, a Ute, in 1921; (bottom) Flute #242, made by John Spear, a Nebraska Winnebago, 1922. Miller Flute Collection, Music Division. (JAG, RS)

56. Ferdinand Joseph "Jelly Roll" Morton (1885–1941). "Frog-i-More Rag." Manuscript music. Music Division; 78-rpm Paramount recording and a hand-colored photograph of Morton. Nesuhi Ertegun Collection of Jelly Roll Morton Recordings, Motion Picture, Broadcasting and Recorded Sound Division. (PW, SB)

57. George Gershwin (1898–1937), Ira Gershwin (1896–1983), and DuBose Heyward (1885–1940). Introduction to *Porgy and Bess,* first page of the autograph full orchestral-vocal score. 1934–35. George and Ira Gershwin Collection, Music Division. (WS)

58. Frank Sinatra (b. 1915). Application for the *Major Bowes Amateur Hour.* 1935. Amateur Hour Collection, Music Division. (SB)

59. Aaron Copland (1900–1990). *Appalachian Spring.* 1944. Manuscript acquired by the Coolidge Foundation in the Library of Congress as part of the terms of the commission. Scripts acquired as part of the Aaron Copland Papers. Music Division. (WS)

60. William P. Gottlieb (b. 1917). *Duke Ellington.* Silver gelatin print, c. 1947. Music Division and Prints and Photographs Division. Gershwin Fund Purchase. (BWB)

61. Igor Stravinsky (1882–1971). *Agon.* 1957. Composer's autograph reduction for two pianos. ML96.S94 CASE, Music Division. Gift of the composer, 1963. (WS)

62. Leonard Bernstein (1918–1990). "Something's Coming" from *West Side Story.* 1957. Composer's manuscript piano-vocal score in pencil. 4 p. Leonard Bernstein Collection, Music

Division. Gift of the composer, 31 December 1957. (RAW)

63. Phillis Wheatley (1753?–1784). *Poems on Various Subjects, Religious and Moral*, by Phillis Wheatley, Negro servant to Mr. John Wheatley of Boston, in New England. London, Printed for A. Bell, Aldgate, and sold by Messrs. Cox and Berry, King-Street, Boston, 1773. American Imprint Collection, 1773. Rare Book and Special Collections Division. Peter Force Purchase. (RFP)

64. Bible. English. Authorized. Selections. *A curious hieroglyphick Bible, or, Select passages in the Old and New Testaments, represented with emblematical figures, for the amusement of youth.* Printed at Worcester, Massachusetts, by Isaiah Thomas and sold wholesale and retail at his bookstore. American Imprint Collection, 1788. Rare Book and Special Collections Division. Purchase. (RFP)

65. Walt Whitman (1819–1892). "O Captain! My Captain!" Proof sheet. 1 p., 11 × 17½ cm. With Whitman's corrections in ink; on the verso, a letter to the printer, dated 9 February 1888. Walt Whitman Miscellaneous Manuscripts Collection, Manuscript Division. (AB)

66. Selections from the Dime Novel Collection, Rare Book and Special Collections Division. (RFP)

67. Lyman Frank Baum (1856–1919). *The Wonderful Wizard of Oz.* Chicago and New York: G. M. Hill, 1900. Juvenile Collection, Rare Book and Special Collections Division. Gift, 1982. (RFP, SJ)

68. *Superman,* number 32. New York: Superman, Inc., Jan.–Feb. 1945. Comic Book Collection, Serial and Government Publications Division. (LWM)

69. Robert Frost (1874–1963). "Dedication." 1961. Typescript with Frost's holograph script corrections in ink and Stewart Udall's holograph printed clarifications in pencil on the last page. 3 p., 28 × 21 ½ cm. Stewart L. Udall Papers, Manuscript Division. (AB)

70. *The Learning Tree* (Warner Bros., 1969). Produced, directed, and written by Gordon Parks. Cinematographer: Burnett Guffey. Music score by Gordon Parks. Frame enlargement from film (copyright deposit, 1972), Motion Picture, Broadcasting and Recorded Sound Division. *The Learning Tree*, manuscript of the novel. Gordon Parks Collection, Manuscript Division. (PGL)

71. Barbara Luck. *Night Street.* Illustrations by Lois Johnson. Vermont: Janus Press, 1993. PS3562 .U2546 N54 1993. Janus Press Collection, Rare Book and Special Collections Division. (TN, AS)

72. Thomas Jefferson (1743–1826). Letter with plan of "maccaroni" machine. 1787. Holograph manuscript in the hand of Thomas Jefferson. Thomas Jefferson Papers, Manuscript Division. (GWG)

73. Charles H. Williamson (1826–1874). *Champions of America.* Albumen silver print, 1865. Prints and Photographs Division. Copyright deposit. (CJ)

74. Marie Martinelo. *The New York Cook Book: A Complete Manual of Cookery, in all its Branches.* New York: James Miller, 1882. TX715 .M368. Bitting Collection, Rare Book and Special Collections Division. (TN, AS)

75. Harry Houdini (1874–1926). Program cover from Scrapbook Number 3, containing pictures, newspaper and magazine clippings, playbills, programs, challenges, promotion, and other materials illustrating the life and professional career of Harry Houdini, the American escapologist. McManus-Young Collection, Rare Book and Special Collections Division. (RFP)

76. Toni Frissell (1907–1988). The Whites and Smiths crossing bridge from Watch Island for tennis at Rum Point. Mrs. James White; granddaughter, Olivia Smith; Mrs. St. John Smith; son, Bunny Smith; Dr. James C. White. Gelatin silver photograph, July 1957. Toni Frissell Collection, Prints and Photographs Division. Gift of the photographer. (BWB)

INDEX

Note: Page numbers in *italics* refer to illustrations.

Action Comics, 148
Adams, Diana, 137
Adams, John, 65, 165
Agon (Stravinsky), *136,* 137
Alexandria, Virginia, map of, 100, *101*
Allaire, Paul A., 9
America First Committee, 51
American Entomology (Say), *86,* 87
Amnesia, and lost identity, 10
Ann-Margret, 131
Anthony, Susan B., 14, 76–77, *76, 77*
Appalachian Spring (Copland), *132,* 133
Architecture, 118–23
Aristotle, 16
Arizona:
    relief map of, *114,* 115
    Tombstone, 36, *37*
Armstrong, Louis, 134
Army recruitment poster, *42,* 43
Arts, *see* Imagination
Augustine, Saint, 13

Bacon, Francis, 162
Balanchine, George, 137
Ballet music, *132,* 133, *136,* 137
Barrett, Mary Ellin, 48
Baseball, *156,* 157
Baskin, Leonard, 154
Baum, L. Frank, 147
Bay Psalm Book, The, 18–19, *18, 19*
Beadle's Dime Novels, 144
Beissel, Johann Conrad, 21
Bell, Alexander Graham, *90,* 91, 92
Berlin, Irving, 48
Berliner, Emile, 92
Bernstein, Leonard, 138
Bible, hieroglyphic, 140, *141*
Bierstadt, Albert, 14
Billington, James H., 6–7
Bill of Rights, 60, 63
Binyon, Laurence, 56
Bitting, Katherine Golden, 158
Black, Hugo, 83
Bolger, Ray, 147

Books:
    American legal tradition in, 60, *61*
    comic, 148, *149*
    cookbooks, 158, *159*
    design of, 154, *154*
    dime novels, 144, *145*
    first in U.S., 18–19, *18, 19*
    Hieroglyphick Bible, 140, *141*
    of Jefferson, *68,* 69, 164, 165
    Oz series of, *146,* 147
    of poetry, 139, *139*
    woodcut illustrations in, 140, *141*
Boone, Pat, 131
Boorstin, Daniel, 35
Bowes, Major, 131
Brady, Mathew, 112
Brinley, George, 23
Broadway musicals, 138
Brooklyn Atlantics, *156,* 157
Brooks, Enoch, 140
Brown v. Board of Education, 59, 82–83, *82, 83,* 84

Callas, Maria, 131
Capitol, U.S., 118, *118, 119, 119*
Carson, Johnny, 17, *54,* 55
Carson, Marion S., 66, 88
Carter, Jack, 47, 131
Champlain, Samuel de, 99
Chase, Salmon, 72
Christian, Mrs. R. E., 111
Church, Frederick Edwin, 14
Church buildings, architecture, 120, *121*
Churchill, Sir Winston, 52–53
Cinema, 10, 17, 147, 152, *152*
Citizen Kane (film), 17
Civil War, U.S., 32, *33*
    and *Appalachian Spring,* 133
    field notebooks, *110,* 111
    and Gettysburg Address, 74
    maps, *110,* 111
    photographer of, 112
Clark, William, 104
Clarkson, Grosvenor, 43
Clay, Henry, 30
Collins, Dorothy, 131
Colorado River, 112, *113, 114,* 115

Columbia Graphophone, *38,* 39
Comic books, 148, *149*
Conrad, Paul, 13, 84, *85*
Conservation techniques, 11, 166–67
Constitution, U.S., 30, 31, 59, 63
Cookbooks, 158, *159*
Coolidge, Elizabeth Sprague, 133
Copland, Aaron, 133
Copyright Office, U.S., 6, 144, 148, 164–65
Cornelius, Robert, 88, *89*
Craft, Robert, 137
Creel, George, 43
Cuisine, 158, *159*
Custer, Gen. George Armstrong, 16, 32, *33*

Daguerreotype, 88, *89*
Dance, and music, *132,* 133, *136,* 137, 138
Daye, Stephen, 18
Declaration of Independence, 15, 59, 62–63, *64,* 65, 66, *67,* 74
Declaration of Rights, Virginia, 62–63, *62, 63*
"Dedication" (Frost), *150,* 151
Denslow, W. W., 147
Detective Comics, 148
Dickson, W.K.L., 95
Dime novels, 144, *145*
District of Columbia:
    map, *102,* 103
    slave law, 70, *71*
Doctor Faustus (Marlowe), 47
Doktor Faustus (Mann), 21
Drobish, H. E., 44
Dufief, N. G., 69
Dunlap, John, 66

Earp brothers, 36
Eastman Kodak, 95
Edison, Thomas A., 39, 92, 95
Eliot, T. S., 55
Ellington, Duke, 134, *135*
Ely, Timothy, 154
Emancipation Proclamation, 72–73, *72, 73*
Emergency Relief Administration, 44
Emmet, Linda Louise, 48
Episcopal Church, 120
Ewell, Richard, 111

Famous First Facts series, 51

Farm Security Administration (FSA), 44, *45*, 152

Federal Theatre Project (FTP), 16, *46*, 47

Fewkes, Jesse Walter, *38*, 39

Fight for Freedom Committee, 51

Film, 10, 17, 147, 152, *152*

Fire insurance maps, 36, *37*

Fitzgerald, Ella, 134

Flag, pledge of allegiance to, 80

Flagg, James Montgomery, 43

Flutes, *126*, 127

Flying machines, 96, *97*

Force, Peter, 22, 139

Fowle, Zechariah, 140

Frankfurter, Felix, 82–83

Franklin, Benjamin, 16, 21, 65, 69, 139

Frank Starr's American Novels, 144

Frissell, Toni, 162

"Frog-i-More Rag," 128, *129*

Frost, Robert, 151, *151*

Gallatin, Albert, 104

Gardner, Alexander, 112

Garland, Judy, 147

General Laws of the Inhabitants of the Jurisdiction of New-Plimouth, 60

Geological Surveys, U.S., 112

George III, king of England, 66

Gershwin, George, 130

Gershwin, Ira, 130, 134

Gershwin, Leonore, 134

Gershwin, Rose, 130

Gettysburg Address, 15, 59, 74–75, *74*, *75*

Gibson, Charles Dana, 43

Globes, *106*, 107

Gobitas, William, 14, 59, 80, *81*

"God Bless America" (Berlin), 48, *49*

Goddard, Paul Beck, 88

Gordon, John B., 111

Gottlieb, William, 134

Goudy, Frederic, 154

Gousha Company, The H. M., 115

Government, 59

    Bill of Rights, 60, 63

    Constitution, 30, 31, 59, 63

    Declaration of Independence, 15, 59, 62–63, *64*, 65, 66, *67*, 74

    Supreme Court, 59, 80, *81*, 82–83, 84

Graham, Martha, 133

Gramophone, 92, *93*

Graphophone, *38*, 39

Groucho Letters, The, 55

Haley, Jack, 147

Hallet, Stephen, 118

Hammerstein, Oscar, 138

Hammon, Briton, 23

Hancock, John, 24, 66

Harriman, W. Averell, 52–53

Harrisse, Henry, 99

Hastings, Selina, Countess of Huntingdon, 139

Hawthorne, Nathaniel, 60

Hay, John, 75

Hayne, Robert Y., 30

Hemenway expedition, 39

Heming, James, 155

Heyward, Dorothy, 130

Heyward, DuBose, 130

Hieroglyphick Bible, 140, *141*

History, 16–57

    as memory, 13, 16–17

    oral, 128

    preservation of, 10–11, 166–67

    process of, 15

Hitler, Adolf, 52

"Hoboken Four," 131

Holliday, Doc, 36

Holmes, Oliver Wendell, 82–83

Hotchkiss, Jedediah, 111

Houdini, Harry, *160*, 161

Houseman, John, 16

Hubbard, Mabel, 91

Hymnals, 18–19, *18*, *19*, 20, 21

Illuminated musical manuscripts, 20, 21

Imagination, 117–63

    architecture, 118–23

    art, 140, *141*

    books, 140, *141*, 154, *154*

    inventions, 155, *155*

    magic, 161

    music, 124–38

    poetry, 139, *139*, *142*, 143, *150*, 151

Ingrahm, Prentiss, 144

Inventions, 88–97:

    cylinder recordings, *38*, 39, 92

    flying machine, 96, 97

    "Maccaroni" machine, 155, *155*

    motion pictures, *94*, 95

    music machines, 92, *93*

    telephone, *90*, 91

Irwin P. Beadle & Company, 144

Isham, Mary Lincoln, 35

Jackson, Andrew, 30

Jackson, Thomas J. "Stonewall," 111

Janus Press, 154

Jazz, 128, *129*, 134

Jefferson, Thomas, 103, 104, 118

    and architecture, 118

    and the arts, 117

    and Declaration of Independence, 15, 62, 65

    inventions of, 155, *155*

    library of, 12, 59, *68*, 69, 164, 165

    on preservation of history, 10–11, 15–17

Jehovah's Witnesses, 80

Jews, equal status to, 27

Johnson, Lois, 154

Johnson, Lyndon B., 84

Josephs, Noel, 39

Kane, Joseph Nathan, 51

Kennedy, John F., 84, 151

Kinetograph, 95

King, Clarence, 112

King, Nicholas, 104

Kirstein, Lincoln, 137

Knight, Gladys, 131

Kresa, Helmy, 48

Kundera, Milan, 10

Lahr, Bert, 147

Lange, Dorothea, 44

Latrobe, Benjamin Henry, 118

Laurents, Arthur, 138

Law, 14

    Anthony case, 14, 76–77, *76*, *77*

    Brown case, 59, 82–83, *82*, *83*, 84

    Constitution, 30, 31, 59, 63

    Gobitis case, 14, 59, 80, *81*

    legal code, 60, *61*

    slave code, 70, *71*

    Supreme Court, 59, 80, *81*, 82–83, 84

Learning Tree, The (Parks), 152, *152*, *153*

Lee, Gen. Robert E., 32, 111

Lee, Thomas Ludwell, 62, 63

Legge, William, Earl of Dartmouth, 139

L'Enfant, Pierre-Charles, 103

Lewis, Jerry, 55

Lewis, Meriwether, 104

Lewis and Clark expedition, 12, 14, 104, *105*

Library of Congress:

    Aaron Copland Collection, 133

    acquisitions of, 164–65

    American Imprint Collection, 19

    Archive of Recorded Poetry and Literature, 151

Armed Forces Radio and Television Service Collection, 51
Bell Papers, 91
Bible Collection, 140
breadth of collections of, 12–13
Broadside Collection, 66
cataloguing system for, 11
Coolidge Auditorium, 133
Copyright Office, 6, 144, 148, 164–65
Elizabeth Pennell Collection, 158
Elizabeth Sprague Coolidge Foundation, 133
Federal Theatre Project Archives, 47
Gershwin® Collection, 130
Gordon Parks Collection, 152
Gottlieb Photographic Collection, 134
Houdini Collection, 161
Irving Berlin Collection, 48
Katherine Golden Bitting Collection, 158
McManus-Young Collection, 161
main reading room, *Title Page*
Manuscript Division, 55, 108, 111
Marion S. Carson Collection, 66, 88
Miller Flute Collection, 127
Motion Picture, Broadcasting and Recorded Sound Division, 51
mural panels for, *78*, 79
Music Division, 127, 128, 134
NAACP Legal Defense Fund Collection, 84
National Film Preservation Registry, 152
NBC Radio Collection, *50*, 51
Nesuhi Ertegun Collection, 128
object list, 168–72
origins of, 6, 11, 69, 164
Papers of the Vietnam Veterans Memorial Fund, 56
Peter Force Collection, 22, 139
preservation in, 166–67
Rare Book and Special Collections Division, 154, 158
Robert Todd Lincoln Papers, 31
Thurgood Marshall Papers, 84
Lin, Maya, 56, *57*
Lincoln, Abraham:
    campaign banner of, 28, *29*
    Emancipation Proclamation of, 72–73, *72, 73*
    Gettysburg Address of, 15, 59, 74–75, *74, 75*
    inaugural address of, 30–31, *30, 31*
    pocket contents of, 12, *34*, 35
    and slave law, 70
    Whitman's tribute to, *142*, 143
Lincoln, Mary Todd, 35
Lincoln, Robert Todd, 31

Livermore, George, 19, 139
Livingston, Robert, 65
Lomax, Alan, 128
Louisiana Purchase, 14
Luck, Barbara, 154

"Maccaroni" machine, plans for, 155, *155*
McClellan, Gen. George, 32
Magic, 161
Major Bowes' Amateur Hour, 131
Malaeska (Stephens), 144, *145*
Mann, Thomas, 21
Maps, 14, 15, 98–115
    Alexandria, Virginia, 100, *101*
    Civil War, *110*, 111
    globes, *106*, 107
    Lewis and Clark Expedition, 104, *105*
    New England, *98*, 99
    on powder horn, 22
    relief, *114*, 115
    Tombstone, Arizona, 36, *37*
    Washington, D.C., *102*, 103
    Wisconsin, 108, *109*
Marey, Étienne-Jules, 95
Marlowe, Christopher, 47
Marshall, Thurgood, 13, 14, 84, *85*
Martinelo, Marie, 158
Marx, Groucho, 17, *54*, 55
Mason, George, 62, 63
Memory, *see* History
Merrill, Robert, 131
Meyer, E. R., 147
Migrant laborers, 44, *45*
Miller, Dayton C., 127
Minerva (Vedder), 8
Mitchell, Arthur, 137
Monk, Thelonius, 134
Moorhead, Scipio, 139
Morton, Ferdinand Joseph "Jelly Roll," 128, *129*
Motion pictures, *94*, 95
Mumford, L. Quincy, 55
Murrow, Edward R., 55
Music, 14, 117, 124–38
    auditions, 131, *131*
    ballet, *132*, 133, *136*, 137
    Broadway musicals, 138
    cylinder recordings, *38*, 39, 92
    and dance, *132*, 133, *136*, 137, 138
    flutes, *126*, 127
    hymnals, 18–19, *18, 19*, 20, 21
    illuminated manuscript, *20*, 21

jazz, 128, *129*, 134
    machines for playing, 39, 92, *93*
    march, 124, *125*
    Native American, 39
    Pulitzer Prize in, 133
    sheet, 48, *49*
Muybridge, Eadweard, 95
My Fair Lady (Rodgers), 138

NAACP, 82–83, 84
Native Americans:
    in dime novels, 144
    in eastern Wisconsin, 108, *109*
    flutes of, *126*, 127
    music of, 39
NBC, 15, 51
New Harmony, Indiana, 87
New York City Ballet, 137
New York Cook Book, The (Martinelo), 158, *159*
Nicolay, John, 74, 75
Night Street (Luck), 154, *154*

Object list, 168–72
"O Captain! My Captain" (Whitman), *142*, 143
O.K. Corral, 36, *37*
Oral history, 128
O'Sullivan, Timothy, 112
Ott, Fred, *94*, 95
Owen, Robert, 87

Paramount Theater, New York, 134, *135*
Parks, Gordon, 152
Peale, Titian Ramsay, 87
Pearl Harbor, bombing of, 51
Pennell, Elizabeth, 158
Personal moments, and history, 17
Peters, Elizabeth Irving, 48
Petit, Adrien, 155
Philosophy (reason), 59–115
Photographs:
    of Civil War, 112
    of Colorado River, 112, *113*
    daguerreotype, 88, *89*
    endless summer, 162, *163*
    of flying machine, 96, 97
    in FSA collection, 44, *45*
    of migrant laborers, 44, *45*
    motion pictures, *94*, 95
    photojournalism, 134, *135*
Poetry, 139, *139*, *142*, 143, 150, *151*
Porgy and Bess (Gershwin), 130, *130*

Powder horn, 22, *22*
Publishing, *see* Books
Puritans, hymnal of, 18–19, *18, 19*

Queen, James, 88

Radio:
auditions for, 131, *131*
broadcast collection, *50,* 51
Famous First Facts series, 51
Ramsay, Allan, 69
Reason, 59–115
government, 59–85
inventions, 59, 88–97
maps, 98–115
science, 59, 87
Relief map, of Arizona, *114,* 115
Religion, 14, 16, 59
Bay Psalm Book, 18–19, *18, 19*
church design, 120, *121*
Episcopal Church, 120
equality for Jews, *26, 27*
hieroglyphic Bible, 140, *141*
Jehovah's Witnesses, 80, *81*
and pledge of allegiance to the flag, 80, *81*
Puritans, 18
Seventh-Day Baptists, 21
Resnick, Regina, 131
Robbins, Jerome, 138
Robert-Houdin, Jean-Eugéne, 161
Rodgers, Richard, 138
Rogers, Bruce, 154
Roosevelt, Franklin D., 43, 47, 52–53
Roosevelt, Theodore, 13, 40, *41*
Rural Architecture (Upjohn), 120
Ruskin, John, 12

St. Lawrence River, 162, *163*
Sanborn Map Company, 36
Say, Thomas, 87
Sayers, Isabelle S., 92
Schoolcraft, Henry Rowe, 108
School segregation, 82–83, 84
Science, 59
Seixas, Moses, 27
Selmore, Peter, 39
Seventh-Day Baptists, 21
Seward, William H., 31
Sharpe, Grenville, 139
Shelton, Hal, 14, 115
Sheridan, Gen. Philip, 32
Sherman, Roger, 65

Short, William, 155
Sills, Beverly, 131
Sinatra, Frank, 131
Slave narrative, 23, *23*
Slavery, 30–31
code of, 70, *71*
Emancipation Proclamation, 72–73, *72, 73*
Smith, Abby, 164–65
Smith, John Rubens, 119
Smith, Kate, 48
"Something's Coming" (Bernstein), 138, *138*
Sondheim, Stephen, 138
Sousa, John Philip, 92, 124
Sports, 117
baseball, *156, 157*
summer vacation, 162, *163*
Stalin, Joseph, 52–53
Stanton, Edwin, 72
Starr, Frank, 144
"Stars and Stripes Forever" (Sousa), 92, *93*
Stephens, Ann A., 144
Stern, Alfred Whital, 35
Storer, John, 123
Stravinsky, Igor, 137
Street & Smith, 144
Stryker, Roy, 44
Superman, 148, *149*
Supreme Court, U.S., 59, 80, *81,* 82–83, 84

Tarzan, 148
Taylor, Paul, 44
Texan Trailer, The (Ingrahm), 144, *145*
Thomas, Isaiah, 140
Thompson, Ruth Plumly, 147
Thomson, Charles, 24
Thornton, John, 139
Thornton, William, 118
Tombstone, Arizona, map, 36, *37*
Tonight Show, The, 54, 55

Udall, Stewart L., 151
Unbearable Lightness of Being, The, 10
Uncle Sam, *42,* 43
Upjohn, Richard, 120

Van Sinderen, Annie Jean, 19
Van Vliet, Claire, 154
Vedder, Elihu, 8, 59, 79
Vietnam Veterans Memorial, 56, *57*
Virginia, Declaration of Rights, 62–63, *62, 63*
Volkov, Alexander, 147
Volta Laboratory, 92

Walker, Donald D., 123
Wanser, Heather, *167*
Warren, Earl, 82–83, 84
Washington, George, 16, 66, 103
and architecture, 118
commission of, 24, *25*
congratulatory address to, *26, 27*
as surveyor, 14, 100, *101*
Washington, Martha "Patsy," 24
Watchtower Society, Jehovah's Witnesses, 80
Watson, Thomas A., 91
Waud, Alfred, 32
Webern, Anton, 137
Webster, Daniel, 30
Weiss, Ehrich (Houdini), *160,* 161
Welles, Orson, 16–17, *46,* 47
Welsh, Howard, 107
West, John, 100
West, Lawrence, 100
West Side Story (Bernstein), 138
Wheatley, Phillis, 139, *139*
Wheeler, Lt. George, 112
Wheelock, Matthew, 69
White, Alfred, 19
Whitman, Walt, *142,* 143
Williamson, Charles H., 157
Wills, David, 75
Wills, George, 16–17, 59, 117
Wilson, Harold F., 107
Wilson, James, 107
Wilson, Samuel "Uncle Sam," 43
Wisconsin, Indian settlements in, 108, *109*
Women's suffrage, 76–77
Wonderful Wizard of Oz, The (Baum), *146,* 147
Wonder Woman, 148
Works Progress Administration (WPA), 16, 23, 47
World War II:
and "God Bless America," 48
Moscow conference, 52–53
Pearl Harbor bombed in, 51
poster, 43
radio collections of, 51
Wright, Frank Lloyd, 117, 123
Wright brothers, 96, 97
Wythe, George, 11

Yip, Yip, Yaphank (Berlin), 48